A CERTIFIED TUCSON CITY OF GASTRONOMY RECOMMENDED COOKBOOK

United Nations
Educational, Scientific and
Cultural Organization

Designated
UNESCO Creative City
in 2015

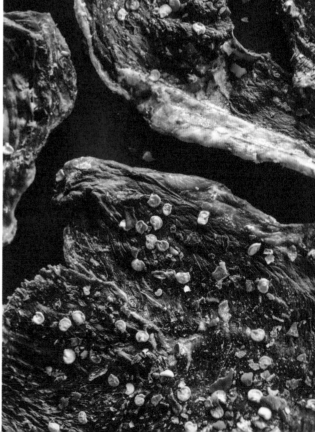

TASTE OF TUCSON

SONORAN-STYLE RECIPES INSPIRED BY THE
RICH CULTURE OF SOUTHERN ARIZONA

JACKIE ALPERS

WEST
MARGIN
PRESS

Dedication

This book is dedicated to all the Tucson chefs, past and present, who have made this city the culinary powerhouse it is today. They have taught me so much, and I hope to share some of what I have learned with all of you.

Editor: Charlotte Beal and Jennifer Newens
Proofreader: Jessica Gould
Indexer: Elizabeth Parson

Library of Congress Control Number: 2019952327

ISBN: 9781513262567 (hardbound)
      9781513262376 (e-book)

Printed in China
4 5

Cover recipe was developed and styled by Erika Mattson Munoz of Seis Kitchen.

Additional image credits: Cover, pages 120 and 127 Jackie Alpers/Photo Courtesy of Food Network; pages 6, 11, 118 Jason Willis; page 117 Michael B. Hultquist/Lerua's Fine Mexican Food

Published by West Margin Press

WEST
MARGIN
PRESS

WestMarginPress.com

Proudly distributed by Ingram Publisher Services

WEST MARGIN PRESS
Publishing Director: Jennifer Newens
Marketing Manager: Angela Zbornik
Project Specialist: Gabrielle Maudiere
Editor: Olivia Ngai
Design & Production: Rachel Lopez Metzger
Design Intern: Gloria Boadwee

While some of the chefs featured in this book are also on the Taste of Tucson food tour, neither this book nor its author are affiliated with the Taste of Tucson food tour. If you are interested in taking the tour and learning more about the history of Tucson, please visit: www.tasteoftucsondowntown.com

Contents

My Story

When I was twenty-five, I decided that I needed to find a new place to live. I had graduated from art college the year before and had been biding time in my hometown of Columbus, Ohio, hanging out with my friends in the punk rock scene of the early 1990s.

I was getting a huge amount of parking tickets and took this as a sign that my time in that town was up, so I took a cross-country road trip with my schoolmate, Andy, to figure out where to live. We ended up at a dive motel called The Tiki in a slightly dodgy part of Tucson, Arizona. The Tiki had a tiny pool in the middle of its parking lot, so Andy and I bought a six-pack of Coronas at the Circle K next door and waded in. It was June and 106 degrees.

As I was sitting in that pool drinking my beer in the clear, bright sunlight with the blue, blue sky that went on forever overhead, I decided that this was the place to be.

The first thing I ate in Tucson that night was a big plate of guacamole and chips that Andy and I shared from the Mexican restaurant across the street. The place was oddly named "21." Based on the sign and the dark exterior, I'd kind of thought that it was a strip club.

Within three months, I'd moved to Tucson, and I quickly landed two very different jobs. One was teaching art to kids in an after-school program, and the other, one that surprisingly ended up altering the course of my life, was busing tables and bartending at El Charro Café, the oldest family-owned Mexican restaurant in the U.S.

I was inspired by everything that I learned at El Charro and all the new food I experienced, whether it was a salsa made from a chile pepper that I'd never seen before, or a salad that looked like a volcano prepared in a way I'd never heard of. The Flores family treated me like one of their own. I was bumped up to regular waitstaff and eventually learned how to work cooking in the kitchen.

I began experimenting with Mexican cuisine and local ingredients. I played around with cooking techniques that were completely unfamiliar to me and photographed food and wrote recipes.

But I never forgot where I came from. I never forgot that I was raised a Jewish girl in Ohio who had never tasted much of this food for the first twenty-five years of my life. I like smoked fish and chopped liver and matzo balls. I like Cincinnati chili, and chicken fingers and hot dogs—a lot. My recipes are a culmination of my own experiences, and I hope that this book inspires you to come up with your own creations informed by a culture, a collection of flavors, and an array of cooking techniques that may be new to you as well.

About the Cuisine of Tucson

Tucson is a hot, dusty college town located just sixty miles north of the Mexican border and situated between Santa Fe and Southern California. It boasts both in physicality and style a truly unique cuisine.

Tucson was first in the U.S. to be designated a "City of Gastronomy" by the United Nations Educational, Scientific and Cultural Organization (UNESCO), an agency promoting diversity around the world. Tucson's unparalleled cuisine is influenced by the city's location in the Sonoran Desert and its proximity to Mexico. Over the years, Native American and Hispanic cultures have mixed with generations of settlers who moved to the Southwest looking for a new life.

Like many American cities, Tucson is a patchwork of cultures that began long before the Europeans got here. What's different is the unique and evolving makeup of that patchwork, and how it has grown into a vibrant and thriving community.

Tucson is one of the oldest continually inhabited regions in the world. The Paleo Indians lived here at least 12,000 years ago. They were hunter-gatherers who lived on the edible flora and fauna. When it was time to hunt, they relied more on small game like rabbit and quail than large game that also roamed the region, such as the giant prehistoric ground sloths. Some of these unique native plants and, to a lesser extent, animals are still part of the local cuisine today. (Not the ground sloths—they're extinct.)

Beginning about 4,000 years ago, the Hohokam Indians learned how to grow crops using ditches that collected rainwater and irrigation canals that diverted water from natural waterways.

As time passed, the regional cuisine evolved. Several key turning points had a major impact on Tucson's culinary evolution: the development of irrigation; land wars and Manifest Destiny (this region was ruled by Native cultures, then Mexico, then Spain, then Mexico again. In 1912, it became one of the last territories to join the United States); the railroad, which brought an influx of new settlers (and new foods) in the 1880s; and, finally, higher education and the military, which brought major sources of population and cultural expansion in the 20th century.

Many years later, in 1992, eighty years after Arizona became a state, and twenty-five years after I was born, I came to Tucson.

People used to ask me, in a voice that conveyed some level of astonishment, "Why Tucson?" They don't ask me that anymore (or at least not in the same tone).

Now the secret is out, and Tucson has become well known for how special it is. Not just for the unique flora and fauna and the enviable number of sunny days—it is a place where nature is still held in balance with city life. Where nature is incorporated into not only our cuisine, but in much of our daily lives.

This region is still connected to the past.
To Native cultures.
To Mexico.
To the Spanish.
To early settlers from around the globe, which include Chinese immigrants, who helped build the railroad.

The cuisine and culture are constantly evolving, as they should. People's personal histories have merged with the region and have grown and evolved just as the area has. I want to pay tribute to all the cultures this community was built on.

I didn't start out wanting to teach people how to cook. My main area of creative interest was always integrating words and pictures. This town was the catalyst for me to explore writing and photography, and food and cooking, in a new way. I hope this book inspires you as much as Tucson has inspired me.

ABOUT SONORAN-STYLE FOOD

The cuisine of this region emphasizes its connection to Sonora, a state in Mexico. Though the borders have been redrawn over the years, Sonora (which Tucson was part of until only very recently) remains only sixty miles away.

This cookbook is about inclusion and it is also about diversity. You will see the merging of cultures over time and the way food has progressed in one of the oldest continually inhabited cities in North America.

You have at your fingertips an array of basic dishes that are staples of Sonoran-style Mexican cuisine, as well as dishes that are mix-and-match reinterpretations of the classics, with contributions from the region's most celebrated chefs.

You will gain a foundational knowledge of Sonoran cuisine, but you will also learn how chefs have expanded upon those basics. It is my hope that by the end of this book you will be ready for your own explorations.

TUCSON-AREA CHEFS

All the local chefs featured in this book have contributed to the culinary flavor of this town, winning awards and accolades in the process. I first met most of them while on photography and food writing assignment for various publications over the years, and they are a big part of why I wanted to create this book. Their creativity and dedication to their craft is truly phenomenal.

Tucson boasts hundreds of Mexican restaurants—more than I have seen anywhere else in this country. Part of the reason for this is that Tucson was part of Mexico for much, much longer than it has been part of the United States. Not all these chefs work at Mexican restaurants, but they have all been influenced, as I have, by our proximity to Mexico, by the community as a whole, and by local history and regional ingredients.

CONTRIBUTING CHEFS

Daniel Contreras: El Guero Canelo
Suzana Davila: Café Poca Cosa and
    The Little One
Carlotta Flores and the Flores family:
    El Charro Café
Benjamin Galaz: BK Tacos
Don Guerra: Barrio Bread
Gary Hickey: Charro Steak
Amanda Horton: Desert Provisions
Bryan Keith: Pinnacle Peak Steakhouse
Teresa Matias and the Matias family:
    Mosaic Café
Maria Mazon: BOCA Tacos y Tequila
Isela Mejia: El Sur Restaurant
Erika Mattson Munoz: Seis Kitchen
Travis Peters: The Parish
Janos Wilder: Downtown Kitchen and Cocktails
Patricia Schwabe: Penca
Bruce Yim: Hacienda Del Sol

Tucson History & Timeline

Tucson is one of the oldest continually inhabited communities in the world.

10,000 BCE Paleo and Archaic hunters and gatherers are found to have settled here.

1000 BCE Evidence of agricultural settlements are located near waterways.

200 to 1450 CE Hohokam culture thrives. Pima and Tohono O'odham are their descendants.

~1540 The Coronado Expedition crosses Arizona in search of the "Seven Cities of Gold." Conquistadors are the first to introduce horses and other Old World livestock to the region.

~1650 The first Europeans settle in the region. By then the Hohokam culture had collapsed, perhaps either from the irrigation water becoming highly mineralized or from infighting.

1699 Father Francisco Kino establishes the Mission San Xavier del Bac south of Tucson. Franciscan friars introduce olives, wheat, wine, ranching, and many non-native plant species to the region.

1775 Official birthdate of the City of Tucson. Hugo O'Conor establishes the Tucson Presidio.

1821 Tucson becomes part of Mexico, thereby winning independence from Spain.

1854 The Gadsden Purchase in Tucson, a 29,670-square-mile region of present-day Southern Arizona and Southwestern New Mexico, falls under the jurisdiction of the United States.

1863 Arizona becomes an official territory.

1867 to 1877 Tucson becomes the territorial capital of Arizona.

1880 The Southern Pacific Railroad reaches Tucson. The population climbs to 8,000.

1912 Arizona becomes the forty-eighth state in the Union.

1950 Tucson's population reaches 120,000.

Early 1950s The chimichanga is reportedly invented in Tucson when El Charro proprietor Monica Flin accidentally drops a burro (a larger version of a burrito) into a frying pan filled with hot oil and exclaims, "Chimichanga!" instead of the curse word that she really wanted to say (because children were present).

1960 Tucson's population reaches 220,000.

2015 UNESCO deems Tucson America's first City of Gastronomy, an honor given to towns with important culinary traditions. "The Old Pueblo" (Tucson's nickname) got the nod for its "culturally layered history, a variety of heritage food ingredients, and a continuity of traditional food preparation techniques."

Sonoran-Style Staples

Pantry Items

A typical Sonoran-style pantry is stocked with many specialty items that are used repeatedly to make the typical dishes of the region. Unless otherwise noted, you can order most of the spices, sauces, and dry goods through Amazon.com, Mexgrocer.com, and my website, JackiesHappyPlate.com.

Beef Tripe An edible part of the cow stomach used commonly as an ingredient in menudo.

Bolillo Rolls Bolillo rolls were brought to the New World by Austrian Emperor Maximillian I in the mid-1800s and quickly became very popular in this region. They are softer and slightly sweeter than a demi-baguette (about 6 inches long and 2 inches wide) and are used to make sandwiches (tortas) and mollettes.

Bottled Hot Sauces There are hundreds of regional varieties of hot sauce. Poblano Hot Sauce is made in Tucson and is one of the best. It comes in many varieties. Cholula, Tapatio, Valentina, La Victoria, and good old Frank's RedHot are all excellent choices. I recommend trying as many different varieties as you can in order to determine your favorite.

Chamoy A bottled sweet/salty/sour sauce made from chiles, citrus, and fruit. Use it to flavor raspados, and as a condiment for fresh fruit and snacks. The Mega brand is a popular variety.

Chia Seeds Native Americans have long used the seeds for food, beverages, and medicinal purposes. The seeds come from a beautiful desert wildflower.

Chickpeas Legumes brought to the desert Southwest by the Spanish.

Chipotle Chiles in Adobo Smoky chipotle chiles are canned or jarred in a slightly sweet red sauce. I prefer jarred to canned since I usually use one or two chiles at a time, and the chiles need to be removed from the can and stored in an airtight

Poblano Hot Sauce, made in Tucson.

Chia seeds and their source.

container once opened. The adobo sauce can also be scooped out alone from the chiles and used to flavor sauces and salad dressings.

Duros A popular snack food made from puffed wheat. Buy duros either pre-puffed or as flat pellets that look like dried pasta.

Evaporated Milk A thick, unsweetened milk that has had some of the water removed before canning. Used in both savory dishes and desserts.

Hominy Dried corn that has been soaked in an alkaline solution. The process softens the kernels and adds nutritional value. The hominy is either re-dried, ground into corn masa, or used whole. Fresh hominy is available at some specialty markets, while dried and canned versions are available online and in many major supermarkets.

Lard Lard is making a resurgence and there are now varieties ranging from very expensive and sourced from organic grass-fed cows, to the classic boxed lard that's been around since forever. Choose the one that best fits your needs.

Maggi Jugo Seasoning Sauce Like soy sauce, this is made with fermented wheat protein. It is used to flavor sauces and savory dishes.

Mexican Chorizo A spicy ground sausage with a deep red hue, available in beef, pork, and vegetarian varieties, and which needs to be cooked before serving. It should not to be confused with Spanish chorizo, which is more like salami.

Mexican Crema A savory, slightly salty table cream with a thinner consistency than sour cream. Use as a base for sauces; drizzle or dollop as a topping. The Cacique brand is most commonly available. Look for it in the dairy section or purchase online at Walmart.com or Amazon Fresh.

Olive Oil Originally imported from Europe. Even though the trees were not grown in the region until 1894, olive trees are now commonly found throughout the city.

Red and Green Chiles, Frozen, Chopped, or Pureed Stemmed and deseeded red chiles, chopped, or pureed, are available in the frozen food aisle in

Duros, puffed wheat snack.

Mesquite seed pods, which are dried and ground to make flour.

Sweetened condensed milk (top), evaporated milk (bottom).

Tamarind candies.

many supermarkets and specialty stores. Look for varieties that contain only chiles. Cook before consuming.

RO-TEL Diced Tomatoes and Green Chiles RO-TEL has a bit of a cult following, but it's sometimes difficult to find the cans of chopped tomatoes and chiles east of Texas. Order online if you can't find them locally. There are several varieties and heat levels available.

Sweetened Condensed Milk Like evaporated milk but sweetened. Used mostly in beverages and desserts.

Tamarind Candies Tamarind pulp is coated in a sweet and sour combination of sugar, salt, and chile powders. The candies are most commonly available shaped into ropes or small chunks. Mexgrocer.com offers a huge selection.

Tepary Beans A heritage food found in prehistoric sites in the Tucson mountain basin. The cooked beans have a bit of bite to them, and a nutty, earthy, slightly syrupy flavor. Rancho Gordo is a local favorite with an online shop.

Tortillas For the freshest corn tortillas, look for them in the refrigerated section of your local market. My favorites are La Mesa Tortillas, based in Tucson. They ship authentic flour tortillas worldwide. See the tortilla section (pages 34–35) for more information on buying tortillas.

Vinegars Red wine, apple cider, and balsamic vinegars are all used, with white vinegar being the most common, traditionally.

FLOURS AND GRAINS
In addition to all-purpose flour, you'll need a few specialty flours to make the Barrio Sonoran Sourdough Bread (page 30), as well as the staple corn tortillas that are served with nearly everything in Tucson.

Hard Red Spring Wheat Flour A red-hued wheat flour with a nutty flavor and a relatively higher protein content. Made from heritage grains local to the Sonoran region.

Khorasan Flour A drought-tolerant heritage grain with a nutty flavor and excellent nutritional properties, also called kamut flour.

Masa Harina Flour made from dried corn. Used to make hundreds of dishes, including corn tortillas. Masienda brand is a superior quality masa made from single-origin heirloom corn.

Mesquite Flour Mesquite trees are one of the most common trees in the region. Mesquite flour, made from the dried and ground pods, is high in fiber, free of gluten, and has a slightly sweet taste.

White Sonora Flour This is a heritage wheat flour, brought to the region by the Spanish who tried, only somewhat successfully, to use it to replace corn in tortillas. It gives extra-large flour tortillas their stretchiness.

PRODUCE

An abundance of fresh produce—tomatoes, citrus, onions, herbs, and tropical fruits—is the hallmark of Sonoran-style cuisine. Here are a few items that may take some special effort to find in your local area.

Chiles Chiles were the most common spice used regionally and historically by Native people, and they are an important component in Sonoran-style cuisine to this day. Look for them, fresh and dried, in specialty markets and some supermarkets, or purchase dried versions from online sources. You can also find red and green chile puree frozen in some supermarkets. I go into detail about specific chiles and their uses on pages 23–27.

Nopales—prickly pear cactus paddles.

Lemons Grown in Sonora since the 1730s, lemons were used medicinally by the Spanish as an antidote for poison.

Mexican Limes Also called key limes, these are about one-quarter the size, slightly sweeter, and more acidic than their Persian counterparts. For the recipes in this book, you can use either type of lime. Typically substitute four Mexican limes for one large Persian lime.

Nopales/Nopalitos It's super cool that you can eat the pads and fruit of the prickly pear cactus because it's one of the most commonly found plants in Tucson. Nopales contributed to the survival of native people in this region, not to mention the native wildlife who rely on the cactus for sustenance.

Tomatillos The name is misleading because it translates to "little tomato," and they do look like green tomatoes, but they are not. The fruit is denser, more acidic, and less sweet than tomatoes. To use tomatillos, first peel off the papery husks, then rinse the fruit to remove the skin's sticky coating.

SPICES

If you live in Tucson and are making traditional recipes, your spice cabinet might look a bit different from that of other parts of the country. Here's a glimpse of what you might find there.

Adobo Seasoning This is made from garlic, salt, pepper, oregano, and turmeric. Some blends also have chile powder and/or cumin. Adobo is often used for grilled or braised meats and poultry. There's a recipe for a homemade Adobo Spice Rub on page 29 that's even better than the store-bought version.

Dried Onion Flakes Dehydrated minced onions add complexity to soups and sauces.

Knorr Granulated Chicken- and Beef-Flavor Bouillon A post-war addition to Sonoran cuisine. Use the variety available as loose granules (not a cube) for precise measuring and ease of dissolving.

Lawry's Seasoned Salt Introduced to the general public in 1938, this seasoning blend is a "secret ingredient" used by many Sonoran chefs, contributing to the unique flavor of the regional cuisine.

Mexican-style herbs and spices.

Sonoran Sea Salt.

Mediterranean Oregano Introduced to the region by European settlers and incorporated into Sonoran cuisine, it's part of the mint family of herbs.

Mexican Oregano Related to Mediterranean oregano in name only, Mexican oregano is not really oregano. It's a relative of lemon verbena and imparts a more citrus-based flavor than Mediterranean oregano.

Pico de Gallo Seasoning Blend PicoDeGallo's proprietary blend of piquant chile-lime seasoning that is hotter and more acidic than Tajín (below). Cooks use it to season fresh fruit and vegetables. It's not as readily available as Tajín; order it online at Amazon.com or through their company website.

Pure Chile Powder Look for pure chile powder made only from ground chiles, spelled with an "E," not chili powder spelled with an "I," which is a blend of spices used to make chili (the warm winter soup).

Smoked Spanish Paprika Made in Spain from peppers that are smoked and ground, available in hot or mild varieties.

Sonoran Sea Salt Milled from the Sea of Cortez four hours south of Tucson. It has a high moisture content and unique mineral composition.

Taco Seasoning Blend I am a fan of McCormick Hot Taco Seasoning Blend. I also have my own taco seasoning blend on page 28 that's superior to any purchased taco seasoning, but it's always good to have some pre-made on hand in a pinch.

Tajín Seasoning Blend A brand of chile-lime seasoning made with ground red chiles de árbol, guajillo and pasilla chiles, dehydrated lime juice, and salt. It packs less of a punch than the spicier Pico de Gallo seasoning and is more commonly found at local supermarkets. Use it to season fresh fruits and vegetables.

Mexican-Style Cheese

Asadero

Queso Quesadilla

Oaxaca

Manchego

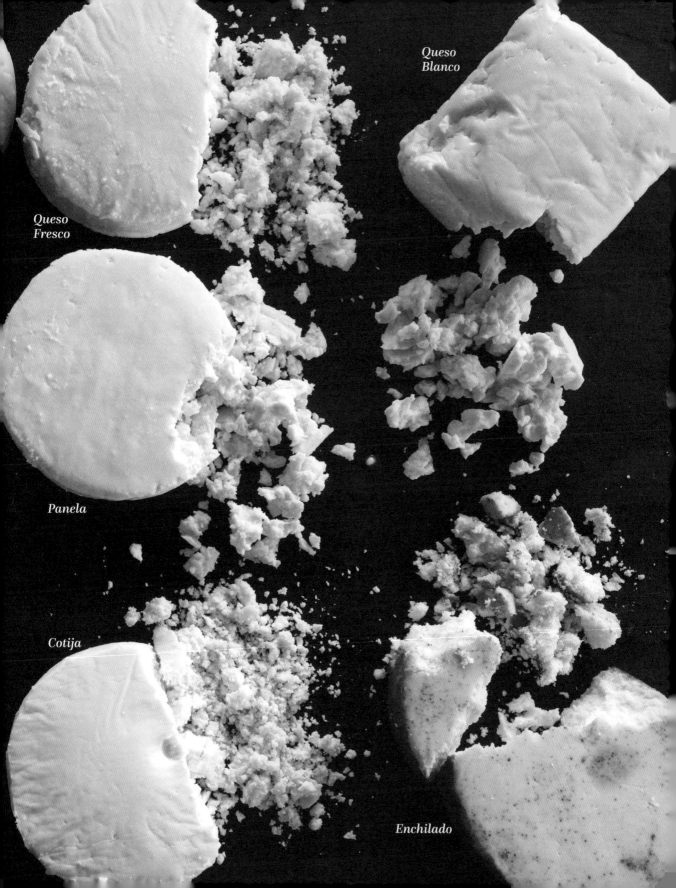

Queso
Blanco

Queso
Fresco

Panela

Cotija

Enchilado

Guide to Mexican-Style Cheese

Sonoran-style cuisine uses cheeses in a multitude of ways.
Texture and flavor are important factors in which cheese to choose for each dish.
Here is a guide to help you choose (see image on pages 20–21).

Asadero A mild, creamy cheese with a velvety texture.

Cotija Crumbly and salty like grated parmesan, used in salads and as a topping.

Enchilado Full-flavored and authentically rolled in paprika to create an iconic red-orange brick-like exterior. Despite the appearance, it has no heat. Crumble it over soup and other savory dishes.

Manchego Melty with a nutty, earthy flavor and a creamy texture.

Mexican-Blend Cheese, Shredded Most commonly consists of finely shredded mild cheddar, Monterey Jack, queso quesadilla, and asadero.

Oaxaca Melty with a buttery flavor and a texture similar to string cheese.

Panela A fresh, crumbly, curd-style, medium-firm cow's milk cheese with a mild flavor that warms when heated but does not melt. Use it to top savory dishes.

Queso Blanco A creamy, semisoft and mild unaged white cheese, similar to ricotta but with more buttery notes. It can be crumbled to balance spicy, heavier dishes or added to soups and salads.

Queso Fresco A soft, fresh cheese that is similar in flavor and texture to a ricotta; this cheese softens but does not melt when heated. Use as a topping or as a stuffing cheese. It can also be sliced or cubed and enjoyed as a snack.

Queso Quesadilla Melty with a nutty, tart flavor and a texture similar to white cheddar.

Chiles

Tucson and the surrounding regions are famous for chiles, which are a staple of the cuisine. There are thousands of chile varieties; these are the ones used in this book (see images on pages 24–25). Fresh chiles are available in the produce section of supermarkets and specialty markets. Consider growing your own if you can't find these varieties locally. Dried chiles are reconstituted before use and commonly used in sauces and soups. NativeSeedsSearch.com sells seeds of many varieties online.

FRESH

Güero (Caribe) Triangular-shaped, pale yellow, thin-skinned chile with a medium heat index, often grilled and served stuffed with cheese. They are also used to make mole amarillo.

Hatch Green chiles grown in New Mexico that ripen in late summer, turning red in early fall. Hatch chiles are a variety of Anaheim chiles that tend to have a hotter heat index.

Jalapeño Most commonly used green, they turn red when ripened. Medium sized and medium heat.

Poblano A large, meaty, dark-green chile, commonly used stuffed and in rellenos. Medium to high heat.

Serrano Small, oblong green or red chiles with a bright, fresh flavor and a medium heat index.

DRIED

Ancho Dried poblano chile with a sweet, fruity flavor and a mild heat level.

Arbol Long, thin, and bright red with a long stem; believed to be derived from the cayenne pepper. Medium heat.

California or New Mexico Dried Anaheim or Hatch chiles with a dark, chocolaty color and very mild heat.

Chiltepin Small chiles the size of a pea yet very hot. They are slightly sweet yet smoky in flavor and are thought to be the oldest species of chiles. They add a slow burn that doesn't overpower the flavor of other ingredients. Crush the dried chiles with your fingers and sprinkle onto dishes, much in the same way as you would use the dried chili flakes common to Italian cuisine.

Chipotle Smoked, dried jalapeños.

Guajillo Dried Mirasol chiles with a bright, slightly acidic flavor and a medium heat level.

Mulato Smoked dried poblano chiles with a rich, complex flavor and a mild heat level. Darker in color than the ancho.

Pasilla Also called a chile negro, pasilla chiles have a raisiny, earthy flavor and mild heat. They're sometimes confused with anchos.

Puya Use as a substitute for guajillo chiles if you want a spicier kick.

Chiltepin chiles.

Dried Chiles

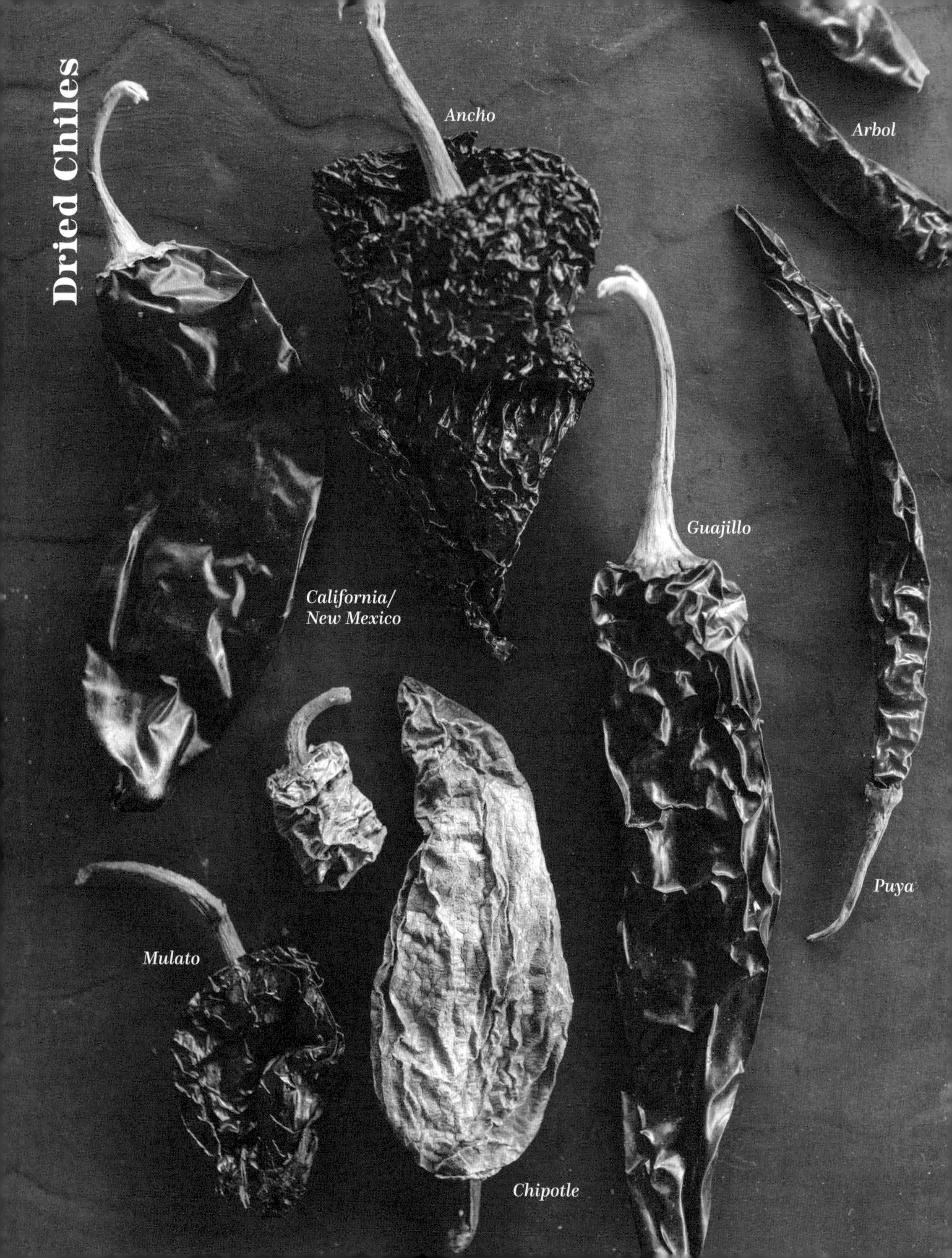

Ancho

Arbol

California/
New Mexico

Guajillo

Puya

Mulato

Chipotle

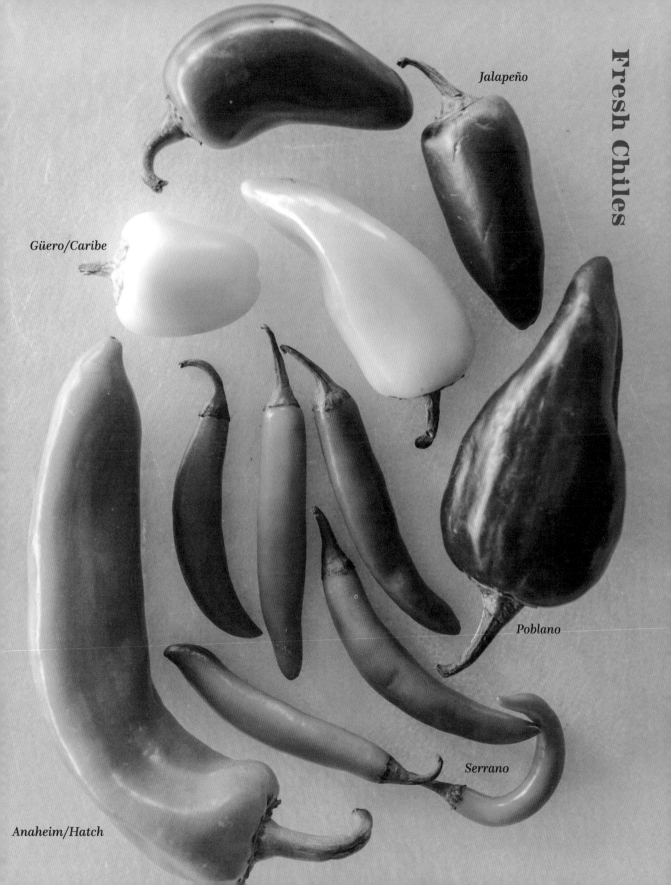

Jalapeño

Fresh Chiles

Güero/Caribe

Poblano

Serrano

Anaheim/Hatch

Make Your Own Chile Powder

YIELDS VARY

Some varieties of chiles can be expensive and/or hard to find, so don't let a treasure trove of chiles go to waste. Amanda Horton, owner of Desert Provisions, showed me how easy it is to dry an abundance of fresh chiles and mill them into chile powder. Use a food dehydrator or the sun to thoroughly dry the chiles, then mill them into a fine powder using a coffee grinder reserved specifically for chile grinding.

Fresh chiles of your choice

Wash chiles and cut them into ¼-inch slices. (Small chiles like chiltepin can be left whole.) Layer them in a food dehydrator. Set it to low. It will take about 12 hours for the chiles to dry thoroughly.

Put the dried chiles in a clean coffee grinder and blend to a fine powder. Store in an airtight container for up to six months.

HOW TO ROAST CHILES

Preheat the broiler or fire up the grill. Wash and dry the chiles. If broiling, place the chiles in a single layer on a baking sheet or comal. If grilling, you can put larger chiles directly on the grate, as close as possible to the heating element. Broil or grill until the skins are charred and blistered, about 10 minutes. Turn the chiles over with tongs and char the other side.

Remove the chiles from the heat and place them in a large heat-safe bowl. Cover the bowl tightly with plastic wrap or foil and let steam for 15 minutes. Peel the skins off the chiles if desired, or leave them on for a more charred taste.

Homemade Seasoning Blends

YIELDS VARY

There are lots of ready-made seasoning blends on the market today. A lot of them are great—made from quality ingredients and very tasty. But I find that there's no substitute for making your own spice blends at home. Here are a few of my go-to staples. Use hot or mild ground chiles depending on your preference.

Jackie's "Taco" Seasoning Blend

Two tablespoons of this replaces one store-bought packet. I put "taco" in quotation marks because even though this is modeled after the popular spice packets, I use it in so much more than tacos.

¼ cup ground chile peppers
3 tablespoons dried onion flakes
1 tablespoon garlic powder
2 teaspoons Sonoran sea salt
2 teaspoons dried Mexican oregano
2 teaspoons hot or mild smoked paprika
1 teaspoon ground coriander
½ teaspoon cayenne pepper

Combine the ground chiles, onion flakes, garlic powder, salt, oregano, paprika, coriander, and cayenne pepper in a sealed airtight container. Store for up to 6 months.

Sea Salt Blend

Use this blend as an all-purpose seasoning. Use chile powder from either single varieties of chiles, or mix different chile varieties into your own custom blends.

1 part Sonoran sea salt
1 part ground chiles

Combine the salt and ground chiles in a sealed airtight container. Store for up to 6 months.

Asada Seasoning Blend

Use to season steaks for Carne Asada (page 115) or as a general seasoning blend.

1½ cups Sonoran sea salt
1 tablespoon dried Mexican oregano
1 tablespoon Santa Cruz Spice Co. red chile powder, or other red Anaheim, New Mexico, or California chile powder
1 tablespoon garlic powder

Combine salt, oregano, chile powder, and garlic powder in an airtight container. Store for up to 6 months.

Jackie's "Taco" Seasoning Blend.

Adobo Spice Rub

Use this rub for the Adobo Pulled Pork (page 125). You can experiment with the seasoning blend in other dishes as well, including grilled meats or vegetables.

6 Persian limes
½ cup ground turmeric
½ cup paprika
½ cup kosher salt
¼ cup New Mexico chile powder
2 tablespoons garlic powder
2 tablespoons ground cumin
1½ tablespoons freshly ground
    black pepper
1 tablespoon crushed red pepper
    flakes
1 tablespoon ground coriander
1 tablespoon dried
    Mediterranean oregano
1 tablespoon mustard powder
1½ teaspoons onion powder
1½ teaspoons ground cinnamon

Finely grate the zest from the limes with a microplane, then place the zest on a paper towel–lined plate. (Save the zested limes for another use.) Let dry uncovered in a warm place overnight.

In a medium bowl, stir together the dried zest with the turmeric, paprika, kosher salt, chile powder, garlic powder, cumin, black pepper, red pepper flakes, coriander, oregano, mustard powder, onion powder, and cinnamon. Store in an airtight container until ready to use, up to 6 months.

Barrio Sonoran Sourdough Bread

MAKES 1 LARGE LOAF

People literally line up around the block at Barrio Bread for Don Guerra's artisan heritage-grain loaves. He says that this bread recipe especially encapsulates the history of grains in Arizona. In ancient times, the indigenous Tohono O'odham people of the Tucson region ate flatbreads with flours made by milling wild mesquite tree pods. Wheat was introduced during the Spanish Colonial period for breads for religious uses. The Spanish colonists also introduced naturally leavened sourdough-style bread. White Sonora wheat is a heritage grain brought to the region by Father Kino. During the Civil War, the Pima Indians and their Hispanic neighbors produced and milled millions of pounds of white Sonora wheat for long-distance trade, and their flour kept thousands of Yankee and Rebel troops from dying of hunger during the last years of that tragic conflict. White Sonora, when grown in the Santa Cruz Valley of Arizona, produces a flour with a relatively high protein content. But it is also low in gluten, making it more agreeable to some gluten-intolerant consumers. In Guerra's recipe, the Hard Red Spring Wheat flour and the kamut support the gluten structure of the Sonora and mesquite flours. All the flours are available online for purchase.

This is a three-day process—excellent bread takes time—and I don't mind! You will need a sourdough starter for this recipe, which you can either get online or from a local bakery. The starter will multiply with your local yeast and bacteria, and morph into its own unique being. A proofing basket helps whisk moisture away from the dough to retain its shape. You can use a glass or ceramic bowl instead. You will also need a large Dutch oven for baking. All the measurements for this recipe are by weight in order to get the exact same quantities of the ingredients as Guerra's. You will need to use a kitchen scale with the measuring units set to grams. You can purchase the flours at Barrio Bread's online store: barriobread.com/grains.html.

continued

FOR THE SOURDOUGH

150 grams sourdough starter

150 grams bread flour, preferably organic

150 grams water

FOR THE BREAD

850 grams water

350 grams prepared sourdough

500 grams White Sonora Wheat flour

250 grams Khorasan (Kamut) flour

200 grams Hard Red Spring Wheat flour

50 grams Mesquite flour

1 tablespoon kosher salt

Pistachio Compound Butter (opposite)

On the first day, prepare the sourdough: In a large bowl, stir together the starter, bread flour, and water. Cover loosely with a kitchen towel and leave at room temperature 8 to 12 hours or overnight.

On the second day, make the dough: Add the 850 grams of water to the sourdough. In another large bowl, whisk all four flours together. Add to the sourdough/water mixture. Stir in 1 tablespoon salt. Allow the dough to rest in the bowl for 30 minutes.

Knead the dough by hand at 2-minute intervals inside the bowl until the dough is smooth. Let the dough rest for 1 hour.

Using your hands, stretch the dough and fold each side of the dough toward the middle. Continue resting and stretching and folding every hour for 3 more hours. If the dough becomes dry and cracked, wet your hands before folding. If the dough seems shiny and wet, add a little more flour.

Flour a work surface. Turn the dough out of the bowl onto the work surface. Work the dough into a rounded shape by tucking the edges under and gently lifting and plumping the dough. Cover the loaf with plastic wrap or cloth and let rest for 30 to 60 minutes.

Place a linen cloth in the bottom of a bowl or a proofing basket and sprinkle it with flour. Place the loaf seam side down on the cloth. Cover with another linen cloth and allow to proof for another 30 to 60 minutes at room temperature. Transfer to the refrigerator for 8 to 12 hours or overnight.

On the third day, bake the bread: Place an empty large Dutch oven inside the oven; preheat oven to 450°F. When the oven is heated, remove the Dutch oven and place it on a heatproof work surface. Take the bowl of dough from the fridge and remove the top cloth. Flip the dough over into the Dutch oven. Peel off the linen cloth and set aside. Using a razor blade or small sharp knife, cut a few slits in the top of the dough. Cover the Dutch oven with its lid.

Bake for 30 minutes with the lid on. Then remove the lid and bake until the crust is golden brown, an additional 15 to 20 minutes. Remove from the oven and flip the loaf onto a cooling rack. Thump the bottom; if you hear a hollow sound, the bread is done. Allow the loaf to cool before slicing.

Serve with the Pistachio Compound Butter.

Pistachio Compound Butter

MAKES 2 BUTTER LOGS

Don Guerra was serving this crunchy nut-infused butter alongside his bread at a farm-to-table event I attended. The second I tasted it I knew I wanted to share it with you all in this book. Thank you to Hacienda Del Sol Guest Ranch Resort Chef Bruce Yim for the recipe. Arizona is one of only three states where pistachio crops are grown in the U.S.

1½ cups shelled unsalted raw pistachios

½ pound unsalted butter, preferably grass-fed, softened

2 tablespoons extra-virgin olive oil

¼ cup (packed) fresh basil leaves

1 garlic clove, peeled

¼ cup freshly grated Parmesan cheese

Juice from ½ lemon (about 1 tablespoon)

Kosher salt and freshly ground black pepper to taste

Preheat the oven to 350°F. Spread the pistachios on a rimmed baking sheet. Toast the nuts in the oven until fragrant and lightly browned, shaking the pan every few minutes to prevent burning, 5 to 10 minutes. Pour onto a plate to cool. When cooled, seal the pistachios in a resealable plastic bag and coarsely smash with a hammer or wooden mallet. Transfer to a medium bowl. Set aside ½ cup of pistachios. Fold the rest into the softened butter.

Put the olive oil, basil, garlic, Parmesan cheese, and lemon juice in the processor; pulse until smooth. Fold into pistachio-butter mixture; season to taste with salt and pepper.

Divide the butter between two pieces of plastic wrap large enough to make two butter logs. Top both with the pistachios, then wrap the plastic wrap over the top, between your hands and the toppings (this will help keep your hands clean), and gently roll into tight logs. Fold in the short end of the plastic wrap to cover the ends. Refrigerate until firm. To serve, unwrap and let soften to a spreadable consistency.

Keeps in the refrigerator for 2 weeks.

Corn Tortillas

MAKES ABOUT 10 TORTILLAS

Corn tortillas are usually 4 to 6 inches in diameter and easy to make. You will need masa harina, which is different from cornmeal or corn flour. Masa is flour that is made from dried corn that has been nixtamalized, or soaked in an alkalized lime solution (from limestone, not the fruit), before it is ground. Nixtamalization makes the corn more nutritious and pliable. Warm water to make the tortillas should be about 100°F, or the hot setting on your faucet, in order to begin blooming the natural flavor of the masa and to fully activate the small bits of pericarp (corn skin) in the masa flour, which help the masa bind naturally.

2 cups masa harina
1½ cups warm water (see note)
½ teaspoon sea salt, or to taste
Vegetable oil for pan

In a large bowl, slowly add the 1½ cups warm water to the masa harina and combine using your hands or a rubber spatula. Knead the masa until no dried powder remains. The dough should be moist to the touch but not tacky, leaving bits of wet masa on your hand and fingers. Add salt to taste. Roll the dough into 1- to 2-inch balls. The exact portion size will depend on the size of your tortilla press. It may take some practice to get the balls the correct size.

Heat a lightly oiled nonstick or cast-iron frying pan or comal over medium-high heat.

Open the tortilla press and lay a piece of plastic wrap over the bottom half. Place a ball of dough on top. Lay another piece of plastic wrap on top of the ball and pull down the press handle to squish the ball flat. If the tortilla sticks to the plastic wrap, add a little more masa to the dough. Lift the bottom piece of plastic wrap with the tortilla on it. Flip the tortilla into the palm of your other hand and slowly peel off the plastic wrap. Then flip it over in the pan. Don't do any of this with too much gusto. The raw tortillas tear and fold over easily.

Heat the tortilla for 30 seconds. Using your fingertips or a set of tongs, flip the tortilla. Cook for another 60 seconds. The tortilla will puff up a bit and turn slightly brown in spots. Remove from the heat, then move on to the next tortilla while you let the first one cool. Tortillas can be stacked and stored in the refrigerator for up to a week and reheated in a dry skillet over medium heat for 30 seconds on each side.

VARIATION: FLAVORED CORN TORTILLAS
Try experimenting with flavoring the tortillas by kneading ½ teaspoon of chile powder or other spices into the prepared dough before shaping.

FLOUR VS. CORN TORTILLAS

I tend to save flour tortillas for a treat and use corn tortillas daily because the nixtamalization process makes corn tortillas nutritionally complete—you could live off corn tortillas and beans if you wanted to. They are only about 60 calories each, and most are wheat and gluten free. Some of the prepackaged "corn" tortillas on the market are mixed with wheat flour, so check the labels.

I've included a corn tortilla recipe in this book because they are easy to make. Flour tortillas, however, require a certain amount of skill and I prefer to leave their preparation to a tortilla professional.

We are lucky to have excellent and widely available handmade flour tortillas here in Tucson. Happily, in this modern era, high-quality flour tortillas are available online for delivery to everyone everywhere. At the time of this book's publication, La Mesa Tortillas in Tucson ships worldwide. Hopefully this trend will continue with other high-quality, hand-stretched tortillas into the future.

I expect that for basic burrito/burro/chimi needs, most people aren't going to want to go through the extra step of making their own flour tortillas. This is a skill that requires a good degree of practice, so I am going to recommend doing the best with what you have. However, you will also want to be able to spot the signs of a good-quality, store-bought tortilla. Namely:
- They shouldn't look too white or too puffy.
- They should be light golden brown in color and have darker brown patches.
- The stack of tortillas should be slightly different sizes and shapes.
- They should have only a few ingredients: white flour, baking powder, shortening, salt, and water.

Beef Jerky

MAKES 8 OUNCES OF DRIED BEEF, OR 1 CUP OF SHREDDED DRIED BEEF

The Sonoran Desert is one of the only places in the world where it's possible to dry beef outside using only the sun. Historically, drying was a necessary way to store and transport food in this environment. Rehydrating dried foods led to unique local cooking techniques. I applied the same basic premise used to make sun-dried beef to this oven-dried beef jerky recipe. Homemade beef jerky trounces the packaged version any day, and it's super easy to make.

1 small head garlic

Juice from 3 Persian limes (about ½ cup)

½ cup water

1 pound ⅛- to ¼-inch (very thin) skirt steaks or bottom round steaks

½ teaspoon Sonoran sea salt

½ teaspoon dried Mexican oregano

1 teaspoon dried onion flakes

Red pepper flakes to taste (optional)

Smash the head of garlic root side up with the side of a chef's knife against a cutting board to separate the cloves, then smash the side of each clove individually to remove the skins and crush the cloves a bit.

Place the garlic cloves, lime juice, and water in a food processor or blender, and pulse until smooth.

Pour the mixture into a large resealable plastic bag and add the beef. Seal well, and marinate in the refrigerator for 4 to 6 hours or overnight.

Preheat the oven to 170°F (a lower oven temperature may not kill any bacteria present in the meat).

Line a baking sheet with foil or a silicone baking mat and top with an oven-safe wire rack. Shake any excess marinade off the beef, lay it on the rack, and season on both sides with Sonoran sea salt, Mexican oregano, dried onion flakes, and red pepper flakes, if using.

Dry the beef in the oven for 6 to 8 hours, depending on the thickness of the beef, turning once about halfway through. It will be a deep brown or burgundy color throughout and just barely chewy. Once thoroughly dried, homemade jerky can be stored in an airtight container for 1 to 2 months and/or shredded and used to make Carne Seca (page 116).

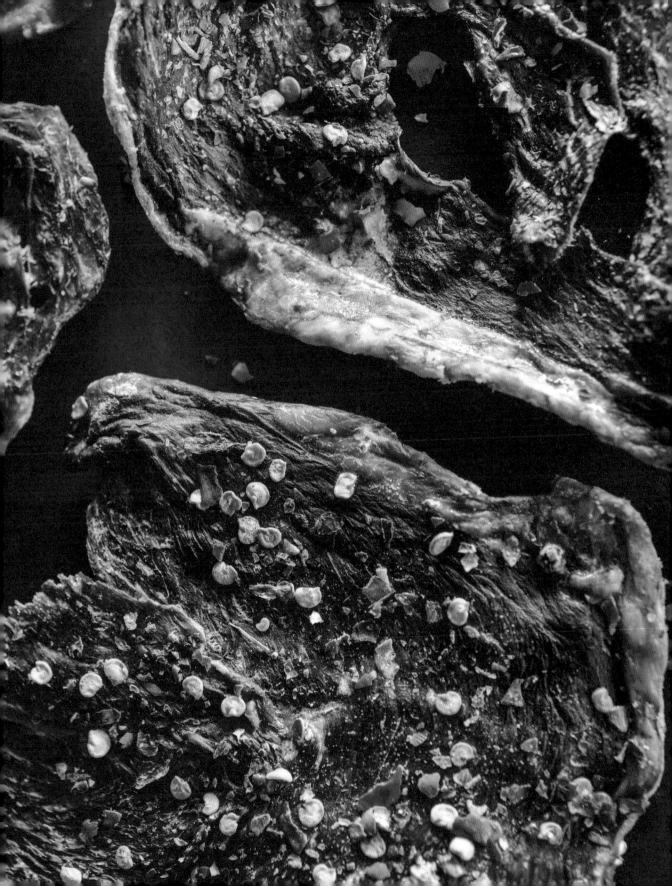

Salsas, Dips & Toppings

Salsa is part of this region's collective identity. Salsa means "sauce" in Spanish, so technically all salsas are sauces. But what is the difference among all the different salsas and sauces you see on the table in Sonoran-style cuisine? First, let's start simple: What makes a salsa? Chiles for sure. Tomatoes mostly, but not always. Onions and garlic usually. And tomatillos or other fruit on occasion. Maybe some citrus or vinegar. That's not a lot of ingredients. However, the devil is in the details! Raw, roasted, or grilled chiles? Fresh or canned tomatoes? Green, white, or red onions? Tucson is eclectic… its evolution from Native American to Spanish to Mexican to U.S. occupancy has influenced the cuisine in a lot of ways, but salsa in its evolution remains a staple.

There are salsa recipes in Tucson that have been passed down for five generations or more. They tend to vary by town, region, family, and more. The following sauces and salsas are a few of my favorites, both classic and modern. I've also included some popular related things like guacamole and pickled vegetables, which are commonly added to Tucson-style dishes.

Chunky Guacamole

MAKES 4 SERVINGS

I expected avocados to be growing all over the place in Arizona, but they don't do well here because the climate is a little too hot. Still, avocados are a major component of the cuisine. Who could even consider any kind of Mexican-based cuisine without the option of a side of "guac"? No one, that's who! One avocado per person is a good general rule for serving size. Once at a party I asked a friend why the guacamole she'd made was the best I'd ever had. Her reply: "The secret is salt." So, don't skimp on the salt, but also, you know… don't go overboard.

4 medium-size avocados

Juice from 4 medium-size lemons, or 10 to 12 Mexican limes (about ⅔ cup)

⅔ cup Pico de Gallo Salsa (page 46), drained of any liquid

½ cup crumbled Cotija cheese

Sea salt to taste

Using a sharp knife, cut around the avocado, starting and ending at the stem. Twist to separate the two halves. Squeeze both halves like you're juicing a lemon to extract the fruit into a bowl. Discard the pit. Pour the lime or lemon juice on top and smash it into the avocado with a fork. Add the pico de gallo, Cotija, and salt. Mix with the fork until well combined. Serve immediately.

CHARRO STEAK'S
OVEN-ROASTED SALSA   CHILTEPIN SALSA OR TACO SAUCE

PICO DE GALLO SALSA   PENCA'S GREEN TOMATILLO SALSA

Charro Steak Restaurant's Oven-Roasted Salsa

MAKES 4 CUPS

The Flores family has been serving salsa at their restaurants for almost 100 years. This version was developed for their steakhouse, and as you might expect, it pairs exceptionally well with grilled meats. Make it the day before you plan to serve it to let the flavors meld.

3 Roma tomatoes

1 white onion, peeled and quartered

2 jalapeño chiles

4 garlic cloves, peeled

1 (16-ounce) can crushed tomatoes

1 cup water

¼ cup fresh cilantro

1 tablespoon sea salt

Preheat oven to 350°F. On a large baking sheet, roast the Roma tomatoes, onions, jalapeños, and garlic for 1 hour or until blackened. Let cool, then place in a food processor or blender. Add crushed tomatoes, water, cilantro, and salt. Blend until smooth. (You can do this in batches if your food processor is too small.) Refrigerate overnight; keeps for 1 week.

Chiltepin Salsa or Taco Sauce

MAKES 6 CUPS

Chiltepin salsa is one of the defining elements of Sonoran food because the bushes that produce the chiles grow wild in parts of Southern Arizona and aren't common to other regions. This is an all-purpose salsa that can be used for dipping, for seasoning, and as a taco sauce. A little goes a long way, so if you prefer a milder salsa, cut the amount of chiles down to a ½ or ¼ tablespoon.

1 cup water

3 garlic cloves, peeled

1 (28-ounce) can crushed tomatoes

¼ cup chopped white onion

¼ cup white vinegar

¼ cup roughly chopped cilantro

2 tablespoons dried Mexican oregano

2 tablespoons olive oil

1 tablespoon dried chiltepin chiles

2 teaspoons sea salt

Put the 1 cup of water and garlic in a blender and puree. Add the tomatoes, onion, vinegar, cilantro, oregano, olive oil, chiles, and salt. Pulse until well combined. Refrigerate for at least an hour to let the flavors meld before serving.

Pico de Gallo Salsa

This salsa is sometimes called salsa fresca or salsa cruda because in Tucson, pico de gallo also refers to big cups of fresh fruit and/or vegetable spears sprinkled with chile powder, lime, and salt (see that recipe on page 166). But this type of chunky salsa is commonly called "pico," so I'm sticking with that. The key to this salsa is the ratio of tomato to onions to chiles. I prefer four parts tomatoes to one part onion and one small serrano chile. Get the best tomatoes you can find. Mealy tomatoes make boring pico.

1½ cups chopped fresh tomatoes
¼ cup finely diced white onion
2 tablespoons finely chopped cilantro
2 tablespoons fresh lime juice
1 serrano chile, finely chopped
½ teaspoon sea salt, or to taste

In a large bowl, stir together tomatoes, onion, cilantro, lime juice, serrano, and salt. Refrigerate for a half hour to let the flavors meld before serving.

SAUCE CONFUSION

Taco sauce is usually blended into a very smooth and slightly thick sauce with the consistency of ketchup. If a sauce is specifically called taco sauce, it is most likely being designated for tacos only and not for dipping tortilla chips into. Salsas tend to be a little chunkier than taco sauce, but most salsas can also be used on top of tacos, for dipping, or as a general condiment. Serve them alongside most of the dishes in this book. Hot sauce doesn't usually contain tomatoes, is bottled, and is made with a combination of chiles, salt, and vinegar.

Penca's Green Tomatillo Salsa

MAKES 2 CUPS

Can green be a flavor? The recipe for this highly coveted, bright and bracing
salsa was developed by Patricia Schwabe for her restaurant Penca, and it really does
taste green. Tomatillos, a native plant that may have been cultivated from weeds,
are commonly mistaken for green tomatoes, but they are instead closely
related to "Chinese lantern" ground cherries and Cape gooseberries.

10 tomatillos
2 serrano chiles, stemmed
1 jalapeño chile, stemmed
2 green onions, roughly chopped
2 cups cilantro leaves
2 teaspoons minced garlic
2 teaspoons dried Mexican
   oregano
1 teaspoon sugar
Sea salt to taste

Remove the husks from the tomatillos and rinse the fruit.
Quarter each tomatillo and add to a food processor or blender.
Add serranos, jalapeño, green onion, cilantro, garlic, oregano,
sugar, and salt. Pulse until well combined. Taste and add salt
and an additional ½ teaspoon of sugar if needed.

Quickly Pickled Things: Red Onions, Jalapeños & Carrots

MAKES 2 CUPS

All three of these pickled vegetables are staples of Sonoran cuisine, so you'll find recipes that call for pickled red onions and/or jalapeños and carrots throughout this book. Mix and match them, or make a batch of each, and experiment with them on everything you eat! Pickling softens the red onion's flavor while giving it a bite of vinegar. Jalapeños are often mixed with carrots and served pickled together.

1½ cups white vinegar

½ cup water

1 tablespoon sea salt

2 cups thinly sliced red onions, jalapeño chiles, and/or carrots

¼ teaspoon dried Mexican oregano

Bring the vinegar, water, and salt to a boil in a medium saucepan. Put the vegetables and oregano in a nonreactive (glass or ceramic) lidded jar. A mason jar is perfect for this. If using glass, put a metal utensil in the empty jar so that the heat doesn't crack it. Remove the boiling liquid from the heat and pour it over the vegetables so that they are totally covered, adding a little more water if needed. Let cool, then cover and refrigerate for at least 4 hours. The jar can be stored in the refrigerator for up to 2 weeks.

Green Enchilada Sauce

MAKES 4 CUPS

In the late summer, chile vendors appear in the parking lot of the supermarket closest to my house, where they roast hundreds of green Anaheim, New Mexico, and/or Hatch chiles in spinning steel cages set over an open fire. I highly recommend roasting your own chiles if you don't have the same opportunity, and I do. There are also roasted chiles available in the frozen foods section of the supermarket, which will work fine in this recipe.

2 cups chopped roasted green chiles, thawed if frozen
4 large garlic cloves, peeled
Half of a small white onion (about 4 ounces)
2 tablespoons all-purpose flour
2 tablespoons olive oil
½ teaspoon sea salt
2 cups vegetable, beef, or chicken broth

Puree the chiles, garlic, onion, flour, oil, and salt in a blender. Scrape into a medium saucepan and stir in broth. Bring to a boil then reduce heat to medium-low and simmer for 20 minutes, stirring occasionally.

Red Enchilada Sauce

MAKES 2 CUPS

In early autumn, roadside stands selling mesquite firewood, pumpkins, and dried red chile ristras suddenly pop up all over town. Though the ristras are most often used for decoration, these are the same varieties of chiles traditionally used to make red enchilada sauce. You can buy the same type of dried red chiles packaged in big bags in the grocery store or online. Look for chiles that still have some elasticity to them. If they easily turn to dust when crushed, they are probably too old. You can still use them, but the flavor will be subdued.

6 chile Colorado (dried Anaheim)
4 dried Chile de Arbol
4 cups boiling water
6 garlic cloves, peeled
2 tablespoons olive oil
3 tablespoons all-purpose or almond flour
1 tablespoon dried Mexican oregano
½ teaspoon sea salt
Chicken, beef, or vegetable stock to thin, if needed

Remove the stems and seeds from the chiles and place the chiles in a large bowl. Pour 4 cups boiling water over the chiles, cover the bowl with plastic wrap, and let steep 15 minutes. Using a slotted spoon, transfer the chiles to a blender. Add the garlic and 2 cups of the steeping water. Pulse until smooth.

Heat olive oil in a large saucepan over medium-low heat. Add chile puree, flour, oregano, and salt. Simmer 10 minutes. Thin with stock to desired consistency, if needed. Adjust seasoning to taste.

El Sur Ranchero Sauce

MAKES 4 CUPS

Ranchero is a smooth, tomato-based sauce that is served warm and is the defining ingredient in both Huevos Rancheros (page 76) and Bistec Ranchero (below), so you can cook up a batch and use it in a variety of dishes to please both meat eaters and vegetarians alike. (Make this vegetarian by using vegetable bouillon instead.) Isela Mejia, who owns El Sur Restaurant, makes the best in town.

3 tablespoons olive or vegetable oil

2 cups diced white onion

3 medium tomatoes, coarsely chopped (about 1 cup)

3 Anaheim chiles, stemmed, seeded, and cut into ½-inch pieces

1 (28-ounce) can tomato puree

¾ cup water

3 tablespoons granulated chicken-flavored bouillon, preferably Knorr brand

3 teaspoons granulated beef-flavored bouillon, preferably Knorr brand

Sea salt and freshly ground black pepper to taste

In a large saucepan or Dutch oven, heat the oil over medium heat. Add the onion, tomatoes, and chiles. Sauté until the vegetables are soft, stirring frequently, 10 to 12 minutes. Stir in the tomato puree. When it starts to boil, add ¾ cup of water and the chicken- and beef-flavored bouillon. Reduce the heat to low and simmer for 5 minutes. If the sauce becomes too thick for your taste, add a bit of water. Add salt and pepper to taste.

EL SUR BISTEC RANCHERO

In a large Dutch oven, heat 1 tablespoon olive oil over medium heat. Add 1 pound skirt or bottom round steak, cut into 1-inch pieces, and sauté until browned and cooked through, about 8 minutes. Pour in 2½ cups El Sur Ranchero Sauce (above) and bring just to a boil. Reduce the heat to medium-low and simmer for 5 minutes. Serve warm with Charro Beans (page 59) or Refried Beans (page 60), warmed corn tortillas, and grilled chiles and/or onions. Makes 4 servings.

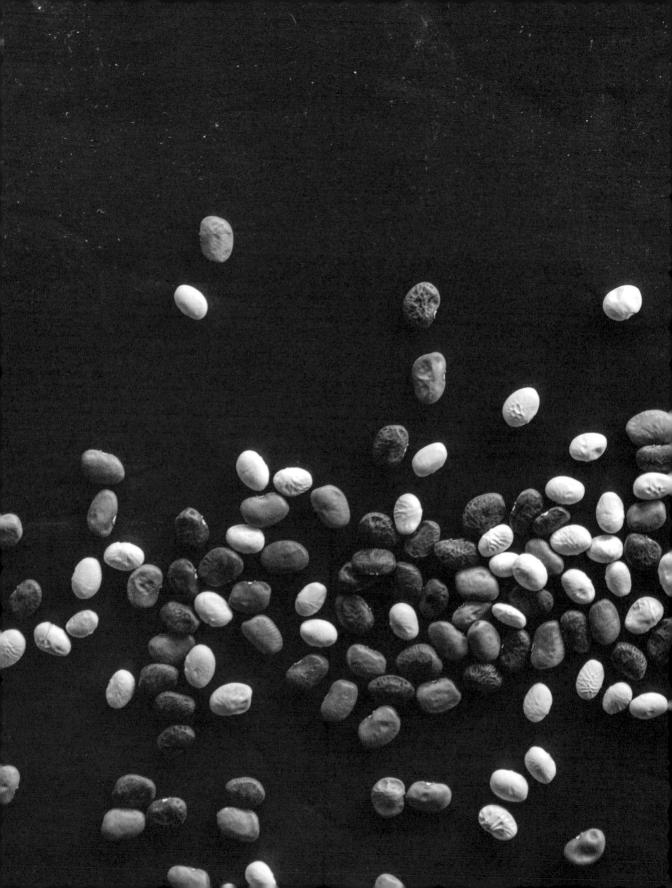

Beans, Rice & Calabacitas

Beans, rice, and calabacitas (squash) are three cornerstones of Sonoran-style cuisine that have multiple uses. Serve them as a side dish with any meal or use them as components in other dishes. One of the key features of Sonoran-style Mexican food is that it's an exercise in creative mixing and matching born from ingenuity and survival that has evolved over the centuries with the help of forward-thinking cooks.

Charro Beans

MAKES 6 TO 8 SERVINGS

These are the saucy, whole pinto beans that you see cowboys (charros) eating off a tin plate by a campfire in movies. Pinto beans cooked this way taste a whole lot better than doctored-up beans from a can (though I do use canned pinto beans for different reasons and situations), and sometimes I'll eat these beans all by themselves as a whole meal with a bit of Cotija cheese on top. I use both onion flakes and fresh onion in this recipe because I think it adds some complexity to the flavor. An entire head of garlic may seem like a lot, but the flavor mellows substantially as it cooks. Dried pinto beans are very economical. You can get a 16-ounce bag for less than the price of a cup of coffee.

1 head garlic

1 (16-ounce) bag dried pinto beans (2 cups)

2 quarts water

2 teaspoons sea salt, or more to taste, preferably Sonoran

½ cup diced fresh tomatoes

¼ cup minced red onion

2 tablespoons red wine vinegar

2 tablespoons dried onion flakes

1 tablespoon dried Mexican oregano

1 tablespoon tomato paste

Smash the head of garlic root side up with the side of a chef's knife against a cutting board to separate the cloves, then smash the side of each clove individually to remove the skins and crush the cloves a bit. Reserve 3 cloves. Coarsely chop the rest.

Rinse the beans and examine them carefully. Remove anything that doesn't look like a pinto bean, such as small rocks or other debris. Pour the beans and about 2 quarts of water into a large Dutch oven or stock pot, making sure to leave 2 inches of water at the top of the beans. Stir in the chopped garlic and 2 teaspoons salt. Bring to a boil over high heat, then reduce the heat to medium and simmer uncovered until the beans are soft, 1½ to 2 hours. If the water evaporates too much during cooking, gently add more water so that the beans are always completely submerged.

DO NOT STIR THE BEANS! Apparently, stirring the bean pot at any point during the 2-hour cooking time is the sign of an unconfident chef, and you don't want the beans to feel insecure about their fate.

Once the beans are soft, mince the remaining 3 garlic cloves and add them to the pot. Stir in the tomatoes, red onion, vinegar, dried onion flakes, oregano, and tomato paste. Simmer uncovered over low heat, stirring occasionally, for 30 minutes to reduce the liquid a bit. You want the beans to be slightly saucy, not soupy. Taste to check the seasoning to see if you need to add more salt, pepper, oregano, or onion flakes, then cover with a heavy lid, remove from heat, and let sit for about 10 minutes to allow the flavors to merge.

Refried Beans

MAKES 4 SERVINGS

Fact: Refried beans (which are only fried once) are better when made with lard. In a pinch, bacon fat makes a good alternative. No vegetable-based oil on the market at the time of publication stands up. For nonvegan vegetarians, a bit of butter mixed in helps. So, my recipe for refried beans includes good old-fashioned lard, but I am also going to give you some choices for vegetarian and vegan options, because I know that beans are a staple for vegetarians who want to eat Mexican, and if we take your beans away there's not a lot left to work with daily. I like my refried beans a little bit chunky, but feel free to make them as smooth as you like.

Some people like to use the back of a firm rubber spatula to smash the beans; some people prefer a potato masher. If you want smooth beans, puree them in a food processor or blender until smooth. The choice is yours. Use prepared Charro Beans for the most from-scratch version or substitute canned pinto beans when you need a shortcut. I know it's a bit of an oxymoron, but using canned whole pinto beans to make refried beans will still taste a whole lot better than refried beans from a can.

IF USING CHARRO BEANS

2 tablespoons lard, bacon fat, butter, or olive oil

2 cups prepared Charro Beans (page 59) in their liquid

Splash of chicken, beef, or vegetable broth (optional)

IF USING CANNED BEANS

2 tablespoons lard, bacon fat, butter, or olive oil

1 (15-ounce) can pinto beans, drained and rinsed

1 tablespoon dried onion flakes

2 garlic cloves, minced

1 teaspoon dried Mexican oregano

Sea salt and freshly ground black pepper to taste

¼ to ½ cup chicken, beef, or vegetable broth

Queso fresco or Cotija cheese for serving

If using charro beans, after the beans have finished sitting for 10 minutes, heat your chosen fat in a large heavy-bottomed skillet over medium heat. Add the prepared beans and smash with the back of a wooden spoon to the desired consistency as you stir and continue to fry them. The beans should be ready as soon as you are done smashing and stirring them. If the beans get too dry, stir in a splash or two of broth.

If using canned beans, heat your chosen fat in a large, heavy-bottomed skillet over medium heat. Add the beans and smash with the back of a wooden spoon to the desired consistency as you stir and continue to fry them. The beans should be ready as soon as you are done smashing and stirring them. Stir in the onion flakes, garlic, and oregano. Add salt and pepper to taste. Stir in enough broth to reach the desired consistency.

If you want very smooth beans, transfer them to a food processor or blender and puree until smooth. Garnish with queso fresco or Cotija before serving.

Fiesta Rice

Like avocados, long-grain rice, grows best in a slightly more tropical climate than Southern Arizona. Yet both are major components of modern Sonoran-style Mexican cuisine. This is a festive and flavorful version of the familiar orange-tinted, Spanish-style rice. To make it vegan, substitute 1 additional tablespoon of olive oil for the butter and use vegetable broth instead of chicken.
Look for Basmati rice grown in California, which, I think, has a superior texture.

1 tablespoon unsalted butter

1 tablespoon olive oil

1 cup long-grain white rice, such as Basmati

½ cup diced red onion

1 garlic clove, peeled and minced

1 (8-ounce) can tomato sauce or puree

1 cup vegetable or chicken broth

⅔ cup frozen peas and carrots, thawed

1 teaspoon dried Mexican oregano

Lawry's Seasoned Salt to taste

Heat the butter and oil in a large saucepan or Dutch oven over medium-high heat. Add the rice and cook until golden brown and toasted, about 3 minutes. Add the onion and garlic and cook for 1 minute. Stir in the tomato sauce and broth. Reduce the heat to medium-low, cover, and simmer for 15 minutes. Stir in the vegetables and oregano. Cover tightly, remove from heat, and let steam until all the liquid is absorbed, 10 to 15 minutes. Fluff with a fork and season to taste with Lawry's Seasoned Salt.

Spicy Green Rice

MAKES 6 TO 8 SERVINGS

This rice is like summer in Tucson—dependably hot, greener than you might expect, and full of complexities that must be experienced to be appreciated. Pair it with milder dishes. Use the green salsa on page 47, or your favorite jarred salsa in a pinch. You can also combine it with chopped or shredded roasted chicken as a filling for tacos and burritos.

1 tablespoon unsalted butter

1 tablespoon olive oil

1 cup long-grain white rice

½ cup dry white wine

2 cups vegetable or chicken stock, divided

1 cup Penca's Green Tomatillo Salsa (page 47)

4 green onions, chopped (about ½ cup)

½ cup green peas, thawed if frozen

1 serrano chile, diced

2 tablespoons dried onion flakes

2 tablespoons minced cilantro

1 teaspoon dried Mexican oregano

Lawry's Seasoned Salt to taste

Freshly ground black pepper to taste

Melt the butter with the oil in a large saucepan over medium-high heat. Add the rice and sauté until lightly browned, about 5 minutes. Stir in the wine and cook for about a minute or until it's evaporated.

Reduce the heat to medium. Pour in 1 cup of the stock and stir until absorbed, about 5 minutes. Pour in the remaining 1 cup of stock and the green salsa. Reduce the heat to medium-low, cover, and simmer until the liquid is absorbed and the rice is soft, 15 minutes. Then stir in the green onions, peas, serrano, onion flakes, cilantro, and oregano. Cover tightly, remove from heat, and let steam for 10 minutes. Season to taste with Lawry's Seasoned Salt and freshly ground black pepper.

Calabacitas con Queso

This cheesy blend of corn, squash, and tomatoes is the third most popular warm Sonoran side dish, after rice and beans. Janos Wilder, who has been awarded Best Chef, Southwest by the James Beard Foundation, has been serving this classic dish for years alongside many of his restaurants' main courses. It is believed that zucchini was developed from species of Native American summer squash brought to Italy by European explorers. For a stand-alone meal, pile a few spoonfuls on top of a warm corn tortilla or stuff inside a quesadilla or burrito.

2 tablespoons canola oil

1 large yellow onion, finely chopped (about 2 cups)

4 medium zucchini and/or yellow summer squash, diced (about 4 cups)

2 tablespoons minced garlic (about 4 large cloves)

2 ears of corn, kernels removed (about 1½ cups)

3 medium tomatoes, roughly chopped (about 2 cups)

2 cups shredded cheddar cheese

1 jalapeño chile, minced (optional)

Sea salt and freshly ground black pepper to taste

Preheat oven to 350°F.

Heat the oil in a large sauté pan over medium heat. Add onions and sauté until softened, stirring occasionally, about 4 minutes. Add the squash and garlic. Sauté until the squash have released most of their liquid and are fairly soft, stirring occasionally, 7 to 10 minutes. Add the corn kernels and sauté 2 minutes. Stir in the tomatoes, cheese, and jalapeño, if using. Season to taste with salt and pepper.

Transfer to a 3-quart casserole dish or individual ramekins, cover with foil, and bake until warmed through, about 35 minutes.

Breakfast Anytime

The unifying factor of Sonoran-style breakfasts are that they are usually egg-centric, the first meal of the day, and accompanied by coffee. You can add an egg to pretty much any of the savory dishes in this book and call it breakfast. That said, there are dishes that are considered local standards. A side of beans and a tortilla along with coffee (or tea) for breakfast is typically accompanied by salsa… lots of salsa. We may eat more chile peppers before 10 A.M. than a lot of people eat in a week. I don't know which came first, the chicken or the egg, but I do know that chickens and their eggs probably arrived in Tucson long before the Conquistadors. Native people were also more likely to eat quail eggs, since the birds wander around cackling like old ladies all over the place here, so feel free to substitute 4 quail eggs for every chicken egg if you have the urge to do so.

Breakfast Burro

MAKES 1 SERVING

Breakfast burros are exceptionally popular at 2 A.M. after a night of barhopping. The signs from locally owned 24-hour drive-through joints dot the night sky all over the city, serving as beacons for the giant burros available inside that are approximately three times larger than a standard-size burrito. Breakfast burritos, or any burros/burritos for that matter, are highly dependent on the quality of the tortilla. Get the biggest and best flour tortilla you can find—12 to 15 inches in diameter is perfect! No meat? No problem! Beans, eggs, cheese, and salsa make a superb breakfast burrito, or use prepared vegetarian chorizo or other meat alternatives. Vegetables? No. Save those for lunch. There is no place for them here. Unless you count salsa as a veggie, then yes. Lots of salsa.

1 large flour tortilla
1 tablespoon unsalted butter
2 eggs

FOR THE FILLINGS
Meat: Optional. Choose one: ½ cup prepared warm chorizo, chopped Carne Seca (page 116), diced Carne Asada (page 115) or diced cooked bacon
Cheese: Yes! The meltier, the better. I use shredded Mexican-blend cheese or sharp cheddar
Beans: Yes! Choose whole (drained) or refried, warmed
Fried potatoes: Optional. Personally, I lean toward none
Salsa: Choose your favorite blended red or green salsa from the book, or combine two or more

Warm the tortilla on a large skillet or in the microwave for 5 to 10 seconds.

Lay the tortilla on a clean, flat work surface. Fold up the bottom third of the warmed tortilla to make a solid work base. Keep warm.

On a griddle or comal, or in a skillet, melt 1 tablespoon of unsalted butter over medium heat. Meanwhile, in a bowl, whisk together the eggs. Add the meat of your choice, if using, and mix it with the eggs. Then pour the egg mixture onto the pan and scramble until the eggs are cooked throughout. Remove from the heat.

Layer the fillings horizontally on the folded area closest to the middle of tortilla, starting with the cheese, followed by the egg mixture, then a layer of beans, and any other fillings. (I like to eat my salsa on the side—biting the end of the burrito first, then pouring the salsa into the open hole, adding in more as I progress.) Roll the base and filling one turn up so that the fold is in the center/widest part of the tortilla. Then, fold the two shorter ends in and roll again until the filling is fully enclosed. Serve right away.

Breakfast Pan Pizza

MAKES 4 TO 6 SERVINGS

Corn masa can be used for more than just tortillas. When mixed with warm water and pressed into the bottom of a skillet, it's about the easiest handmade pizza crust ever. This makes more gravy than you will need. Save the rest to serve with biscuits or sloppy joes.

FOR THE CORN MASA CRUST

½ cup masa harina

⅛ teaspoon sea salt

½ cup very warm water

1 teaspoon olive oil or olive oil spray

FOR THE CHORIZO GRAVY

4 ounces Mexican chorizo

2 tablespoons diced white onion

2 tablespoons all-purpose flour

1 cup whole milk

¼ teaspoon smoked paprika

Freshly ground black pepper to taste

FOR THE TOPPING

2 large eggs

1 tablespoon whole milk

½ cup shredded Mexican-blend cheese

Crushed red pepper flakes (optional)

¼ teaspoon ground sage (optional)

Grated Cotija cheese (optional)

Preheat the oven to 350°F. Lightly oil a 9- to 10-inch oven-safe skillet, preferably cast-iron.

In a mixing bowl, combine the masa harina, salt, and water. Knead until no dried powder remains. The dough should be moist to touch, but not tacky. Roll the dough into a ball. Press into the bottom and up the sides of the skillet to form the crust. Spray or brush lightly with olive oil. Bake for 15 minutes or until lightly golden.

Meanwhile, make the gravy. Heat a large nonstick skillet over medium-high heat. Add the chorizo and onion; cook until the chorizo is browned and crisp, breaking up any large pieces with a spatula, about 5 minutes. Sprinkle the flour over the chorizo mixture and stir until completely absorbed, about 2 minutes more. Reduce the heat to medium-low. Pour in the milk ½ cup at a time, stirring constantly until incorporated, about 5 minutes total. Stir in the smoked paprika and lots of black pepper. Set aside ½ cup of the gravy and keep warm. You can freeze the remaining gravy for up to 2 months or store in the refrigerator for up to 5 days. To reheat, thaw in the refrigerator first, then heat in a saucepan over low heat, stirring occasionally until warmed.

Raise the oven heat to 425°F. Spread ½ cup warm gravy over the crust. In a bowl, beat the eggs and milk with a fork. Pour over the gravy. Arrange the cheese evenly over the top and sprinkle with red pepper flakes and sage, if using. Bake the pizza until puffy and golden brown on top, 12 to 15 minutes. Sprinkle lightly with grated Cotija cheese, if desired, slice, and serve.

VARIATION: CHORIZO SLOPPY JOES

Warm the leftover gravy in a saucepan over medium heat and stir in 2 tablespoons of tomato paste. Slice and toast bolillo rolls, then spoon the gravy over one half and top with the other half to make sandwiches. Makes 2 to 4 servings.

Huevos Rancheros

MAKES 2 SERVINGS

Great Sonoran-style Mexican cuisine is fully dependent on the sum of the quality of its parts. There are recipes for Huevos Rancheros everywhere; there are not recipes for Huevos Rancheros made with Sonoran-style components.

4 corn tortillas (page 34)
2 teaspoons unsalted butter
4 large eggs
1 cup Refried Beans (page 60), warmed
2 cups prepared El Sur Ranchero Sauce (page 53), warmed
½ cup shredded Mexican-blend cheese

Preheat the oven to 350°F.

Add about a teaspoon of water onto a nonstick skillet and warm over medium heat until it sizzles. Toss in the tortillas and heat for a minute or two on each side until slightly toasted. Transfer to an ovenproof plate. Add the butter to the skillet over medium heat. When it's melted, gently crack the eggs on top and fry them until the whites are crispy and the yolks start to set, about 3 minutes.

Meanwhile, cover the tortillas with the warm refried beans, then top each with one of the cooked eggs. Spoon the Ranchero Sauce around the sides of the eggs. Sprinkle the cheese over everything. Put the plate in the oven and bake until the cheese is melted, about 3 minutes.

OVENPROOF PLATES

To tell if your plate is safe to heat in the oven, turn it over and look for an oven icon—or the words "oven safe"—on the underside. Take care not to use too high heat—usually 350°F is the max for plates.

Eggs Diablo

MAKES 2 SERVINGS

Here is another great way to use the El Sur Ranchero Sauce! This time, the eggs are simmered in the sauce and baked in the oven with cheese on top. You'd think that this would taste almost the same as Huevos Rancheros, but the different cooking technique changes the flavors considerably. Pass hot sauce at the table if you like your dish spicy.

1 cup El Sur Ranchero Sauce
(page 53)
4 eggs
Hot sauce (optional)
¼ cup crumbled queso fresco
¼ cup shredded sharp cheddar
cheese
Warm corn or flour tortillas
for serving

Preheat the oven to 350°F.

Heat the ranchero sauce in an ovenproof skillet over medium heat. When the sauce starts to boil, gently crack in the eggs. Simmer until the eggs are set and the yolks have thickened but are not hard, about 5 minutes. Sprinkle the hot sauce, if using, and both cheeses evenly over the top. Transfer the skillet to the oven and bake until the cheese is melted and the eggs are set, 5 to 10 minutes.

Serve straight from the skillet with a large spoon, with the tortillas on the side. Remember to place a trivet on the table under the hot pan.

Molletes

MAKES 2 SERVINGS

These open-faced breakfast sandwiches are made by slathering refried beans onto toasted bolillo rolls and then heaping avocado slices, a fried egg, hot sauce, and lots of cheese on top. If you can't find bolillos at your local bakery, use a sweet French roll instead.

2 bolillo rolls or demi baguette, halved lengthwise
1 cup Refried Beans (page 60), warmed
½ cup crumbled queso fresco
4 fried eggs
1 medium avocado, sliced
Hot sauce to taste
Sea salt and freshly ground black pepper to taste
Chile powder to taste

Preheat the broiler.

Toast the bread until golden brown and then place on a foil-lined baking sheet or toaster oven pan. Heap the beans on top of each bread slice, dividing evenly, then cover with the cheese, again dividing evenly. Place the sandwiches under the broiler or in the toaster oven until the cheese is melted.

Remove the sandwiches from the oven and layer each with 1 fried egg and a few slices of avocado. Season with hot sauce, salt, pepper, and chile powder to taste.

Three-Minute Mug Migas

Even on busy workdays, you can enjoy a Sonoran-style breakfast. Migas are made with eggs, salsa, cheese, and a few tortilla chips, and they can be assembled and cooked up in a mug in your microwave in three minutes or less and eaten on the go! It's easy to confuse migas with chilaquiles. Chilaquiles are heavier on the chips than migas and are more like a meatless lasagna with layers of enchilada sauce, tortilla chips, and cheese. Migas are lighter and the chips are an accent, not the central component.

2 large eggs

¼ cup salsa of choice (I like Penca's Green Tomatillo salsa, page 47), plus more for serving

1 tablespoon Mexican crema, sour cream, or plain Greek yogurt

Large handful of tortilla chips, plus additional for serving

3 tablespoons shredded Mexican-blend cheese

½ avocado, diced

In a large liquid measuring cup, whisk together the eggs, salsa, and crema. Crush the handful of chips into the egg mixture, then fold in the cheese. Pour into a large mug and microwave on high until the eggs are set, 2 to 3 minutes. Top with the diced avocado, extra chips, and a spoonful of additional salsa.

Note: All microwaves cook differently, so check every 30 seconds or so to ensure your migas have not overcooked.

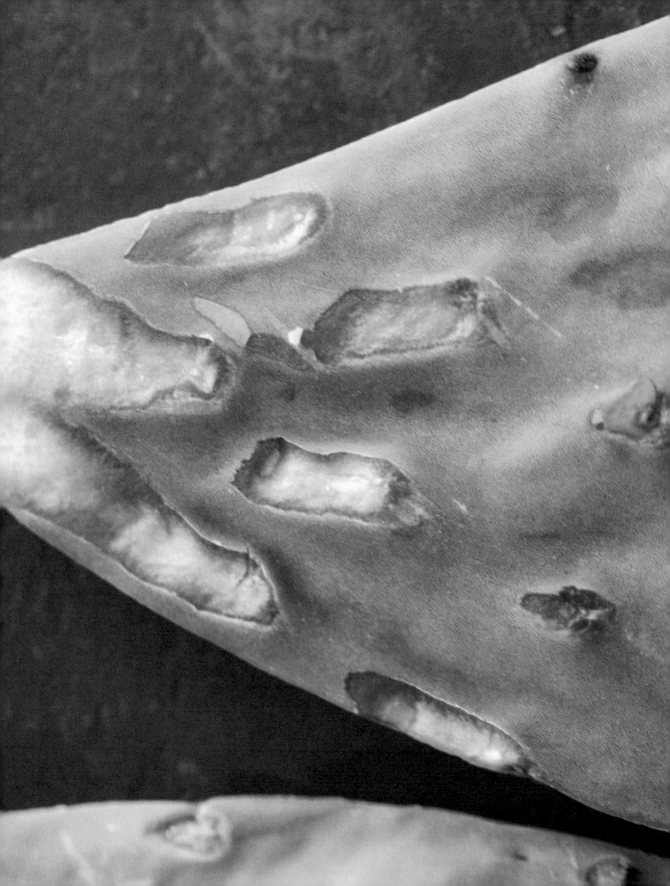

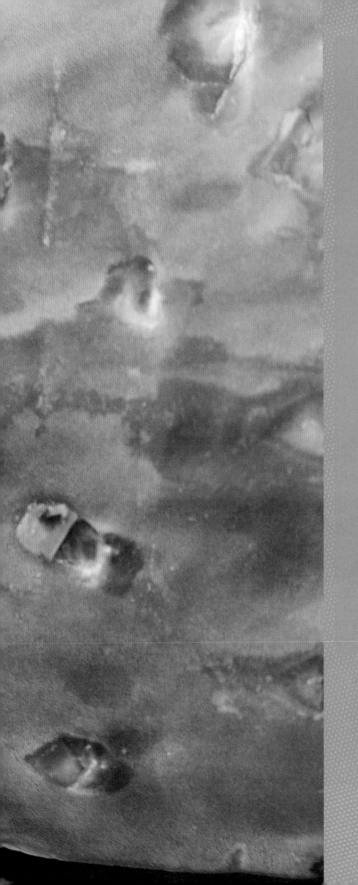

Soups & Salads

Large bowls of both soup and salad are also common main dish meals, served with sides of rice, beans, and tortillas. The desert is hot and dry, and both soup and salad are hydrating, which may contribute to why both are consumed all year round. Tiny salads consisting of shredded or chopped lettuce and a bit of cheese are almost always nestled up against enchiladas and other saucy warm dishes, while a cup of soup is commonly served before a meal and after a communal appetizer, such as a cheese crisp.

Quick & Easy
Chicken Tortilla Soup

MAKES 4 TO 6 SERVINGS

I'd never encountered any of the soups in this book before I moved to Tucson. Tortilla soup has taken the world by storm, and versions are readily available in supermarkets. The Sonoran version of tortilla soup is different from any of the prepackaged versions I've seen. It features crushed tortilla chips and melted cheese anchored in a clear broth seasoned with garlic, green chiles, and Mexican oregano. I've used shredded rotisserie chicken so that it's ready in about 30 minutes—not much longer than heating up soup from a can.

1 tablespoon olive oil

1 tablespoon unsalted butter

1 medium white onion, diced (about 1 cup)

2 cloves garlic, minced

½ cup dry white wine

1 (10-ounce) can RO-TEL tomatoes and chiles, hot or mild variety

3 cups shredded rotisserie chicken, skin removed

4 cups chicken broth or stock

1 tablespoon dried Mexican oregano

1 teaspoon Lawry's Seasoned Salt, plus more to taste

½ teaspoon freshly ground black pepper

⅛ teaspoon ground cumin

1 bay leaf

2 to 3 tablespoons crumbled queso blanco, queso fresco, or Panela cheese per serving

6 tortilla chips per serving, crushed

1 avocado, diced

Crushed dried chiltepin chiles and/or salsa

In a large saucepan or stockpot, heat the olive oil and butter over medium-high heat. Add the onion and garlic and sauté until soft, about 5 minutes. Pour in the wine and cook for 1 minute. Add the RO-TEL and the shredded chicken; cook for about 3 minutes to meld the flavors. Add the broth, oregano, Lawry's Seasoned Salt, pepper, cumin, and bay leaf. Bring to a boil. Reduce the heat to medium and cook, covered, for 20 minutes. Season with additional seasoned salt to taste.

To serve, put 2 to 3 tablespoons of cheese into the bottom of each wide, shallow bowl. Ladle in the soup. Let diners pile on their own crushed tortilla chips and diced avocado. Chiltepin chiles add more heat but less flavor than salsa, so offer both as options.

Caldo de Queso

MAKES 4 SERVINGS

Caldo de Queso is a classic Sonoran-style soup made from potatoes and cheese in a light, milky broth. A similar soup, Cazuela de Carne Seca, is an easy variation, with dried beef (carne seca) replacing the cheese. This is a good example of how you can make two totally different soups by simply swapping out one ingredient. Meat and potatoes are two very North American staples that have become mainstays of Sonoran cuisine as well. Potatoes were brought up from Peru, where they were eaten by and worshiped by the Incas. Serve these soups with crushed dried chiltepin chiles on the side instead of hot sauce for an extra kick that doesn't mask the subtle flavors of the soup.

4 medium Yukon Gold potatoes (about 2 pounds), peeled and quartered

2 medium tomatoes, chopped (about 1 cup)

1 medium white onion, diced (about 1 cup)

1 (7-ounce) can diced green chiles

4 garlic cloves, minced

1 tablespoon dried rosemary

4 cups chicken or vegetable broth

1 (12-ounce) can evaporated milk

1 cup water

Sea salt and freshly ground black pepper to taste

1 cup shredded Manchego, Oaxaca, and/or queso quesadilla

Crushed dried chiltepin chiles and tortillas for serving

Add the potatoes, tomatoes, onion, green chiles, garlic, rosemary, broth, evaporated milk, and 1 cup water to a large saucepan or stockpot. Bring to a boil over high heat, then reduce the heat to medium and simmer until the potatoes are tender when poked with a fork, about 20 minutes. Season to taste with salt and pepper.

Put ¼ cup of the cheese in the bottom of each of 4 bowls, then ladle the soup over the top. Serve with crushed dried chiltepin chiles and warm tortillas.

VARIATION: CAZUELA DE CARNE SECA
Follow the recipe for Caldo de Queso, replacing the cheese with ⅓ cup Carne Seca (page 116).

Teresa's White Menudo

Back in Ohio in the early 1980s, I knew Menudo as a boy band named after a soup I had never tasted, and that both the soup and the band were supposed to be spicy and from Mexico. A lot of what I now know about this traditional tripe soup I learned from Teresa Matias of Teresa's Mosaic Café. Her biggest tip is to buy the best-quality fresh honeycomb tripe you can find. Serve this soup with toasted and buttered bolillo rolls. Try and use fresh hominy if possible. A lot of people think of the soup as a classic hangover cure, which may be why many restaurants only serve this slow-cooking soup on the weekends.

FOR THE TRIPE
1 pound honeycomb tripe
8 cups water

FOR THE SOUP
1½ cups canned or fresh hominy (one 15.5-ounce can), well rinsed
1 medium white onion, chopped (about 1 cup)
3 garlic cloves, peeled and chopped (about 1 tablespoon)
2 green onions, chopped
½ fresh green Anaheim chile, chopped
¼ cup sea salt
Optional garnishes: minced cilantro, minced white onion, crushed chiltepin, and dried Mexican oregano

With your hands, thoroughly clean the tripe under cold running water using a scrubbing motion. Trim the fat from the tripe and dice the tripe into 1-inch pieces. Rinse the diced tripe in a large bowl and drain through a colander, changing the water several times to be sure that the tripe is very clean Add the tripe and the 8 cups water to a large soup pot or Dutch oven. Bring to a boil. Properly cleaned tripe will remain clear when added to boiling water. If the water is not clear, drain the tripe and wash it again before returning it to the boiling water. Reduce the heat to medium and cook, covered, until tender, about 2 hours.

Add the hominy, onion, garlic, green onions, and chile. Allow to boil until the hominy is tender, about 1 hour. Add ¼ cup salt; adjust seasoning to taste.

Ladle into bowls. If desired, garnish with minced cilantro, white onion, crushed Chiltepin chiles, and dried oregano.

VARIATION: TERESA'S RED MENUDO
Follow the White Menudo recipe. At the step when you add the hominy, also add: 1 cup red chile powder, 1 tablespoon garlic powder, and 1 teaspoon dried Mexican oregano.

Matzalbondigas

MAKES 4 TO 8 SERVINGS

Albondigas are small meatballs commonly served in a broth flavored with chiles and vegetables. The dish was brought over to the Sonoran region by the Spanish and is found at restaurants all over town in different iterations, including chicken, turkey, beef, shrimp, and fish. One year, inspired by Passover, I decided to personalize my version of this popular soup by swapping out the meatballs for matzo balls, and Matzalbondigas was born.

FOR THE MATZO BALLS
2 large eggs
2 tablespoons olive oil
1 packet (2½ ounces) matzo ball mix (I use Manischewitz)
1 tablespoon dried onion flakes

FOR THE SOUP
2 tablespoons olive oil
2 celery stalks, diced (about ½ cup)
2 carrots, diced (about ½ cup)
1 small white onion, diced (about ½ cup)
1 cup chopped white button or cremini mushrooms
6 large dried New Mexico chiles
2 dried Guajillo, pasilla, or arbol chiles
8 cups water
5 garlic cloves, peeled
4 cups vegetable or chicken broth or stock
½ cup dry red wine
2 tablespoons chopped cilantro
1 tablespoon dried Mexican oregano
1 tablespoon tomato paste
1 teaspoon sea salt, preferably Sonoran
1 bay leaf
Grated Cotija cheese for garnish

To prepare the matzo ball mixture, whisk together the eggs and olive oil in a medium bowl. Pour in the matzo ball mix and dried onion flakes and stir until well combined. Refrigerate for at least 15 minutes.

To make the soup, heat the olive oil in a large Dutch oven or stockpot over medium heat. Add the celery, carrots, and onion. Sauté until soft, about 10 minutes. Add the mushrooms and continue cooking for 5 more minutes.

Break the stems off the dried chiles and shake out the seeds. Discard the stems and seeds. Boil the chiles in 4 cups of the water until soft, about 12 to 15 minutes. Blend the softened chiles, 1 cup of the cooking water, and garlic in a blender until smooth.

Add the pureed chile mixture to the pot. Add the broth, wine, remaining 4 cups of water, cilantro, oregano, tomato paste, 1 teaspoon salt, and the bay leaf. Bring to a boil over high heat.

Take the matzo ball mixture out of the fridge. Wet your hands and form approximately eight 1½-inch balls, plopping them one by one into the boiling broth after you form them. Cover the pot tightly. Reduce the heat to medium-low and simmer for 20 minutes undisturbed. Remove one matzo ball and cut it in half; the texture should be light and fluffy. If not, continue to simmer for a few more minutes.

To serve, divide the matzo balls among serving bowls and ladle the soup over the top. Garnish with Cotija cheese.

Red Pozole

MAKES 6 TO 8 SERVINGS

This pork and hominy stew is a traditional "low-and-slow" braising recipe. It takes about 3½ hours to cook from start to finish because pork shoulder is a fatty cut of meat that takes a while to break down. But the pork fat is what gives this soup its richness. My Sonoran-style version of this dish is topped with lots of fresh vegetables and citrus for counterbalance.

1 tablespoon olive oil

1 pound pork shoulder, cut into 1-inch pieces

1 medium sized white onion, chopped (about 1 cup)

10 cups water

1 teaspoon sea salt

1 bay leaf

4 dried chiles de arbol

2 dried ancho chiles

2 cups water

8 garlic cloves, peeled

1 (25-ounce) can hominy, drained and rinsed

1 tablespoon dried Mexican oregano

FOR GARNISHING

Shredded cabbage

Chopped cilantro

Sliced radishes

Crushed red pepper flakes

Chopped green onion

Lime or lemon wedges

Sear the pork shoulder with the onions in the olive oil over high heat in a large heavy-lidded Dutch oven or soup pot for 3 to 5 minutes, stirring occasionally to turn the pork pieces, until browned. Add the 10 cups of water, 1 teaspoon salt, and the bay leaf. Bring to a boil. Reduce heat to medium-low. Cook uncovered for 1 hour. Reduce heat to low, cover, and simmer until the pork is fork-tender and beginning to fall apart, about 2 hours more.

Meanwhile, break the stems off the dried chiles and shake out the seeds. Discard the stems and seeds. Bring 2 cups of water and the chiles to a boil in a medium saucepan. Boil until soft, stirring occasionally and submerging any chiles that float to the top, 12 to 15 minutes. Transfer the chiles and their cooking liquid to a blender and add the garlic. Blend until smooth.

Skim off about half of the fat from the broth, if desired. Remove any big pieces of pork that haven't fallen apart with a slotted spoon, roughly chop, and add back to the pot. Add the hominy, Mexican oregano, and chile-garlic puree. Cook uncovered for 20 minutes. Season to taste with salt.

Spoon into bowls. Garnish with cabbage, cilantro, radishes, red pepper flakes, and green onions. Pass lime or lemon wedges to squeeze in juice to taste.

Crema de Aguacate (Cream of Avocado Soup)

MAKES 2 TO 4 SERVINGS

Science says that eating warm soup can help regulate body temperature during the hot summer months, and this bright and light, warm and simple soup can be ready in 20 minutes or less, making it a good choice for weeknight summer meals. Lemon complements the richness of both the half-and-half and avocado perfectly. Even though avocados are not native to the region, they have become an integral part of Sonoran cuisine, and the flavors are now unmistakably Sonoran.

1 (26-ounce) carton chicken broth or stock
3 ripe avocados
Juice from 2 lemons, plus 1 additional sliced lemon for garnish
½ cup half-and-half
¼ cup chopped cilantro, plus more for garnish
Sea salt and freshly ground black pepper to taste

Bring the broth to a boil in a medium pot. Meanwhile, peel, pit, and mash 2 of the avocados.

When the broth comes to a boil, reduce the heat to medium-low. Stir in the mashed avocado and lemon juice; simmer for 5 minutes. Let cool slightly, then blend until smooth using an immersion or traditional blender. Stir in the half-and-half and cilantro. Simmer for an additional 5 to 10 minutes over low heat. While the soup is simmering, peel, pit, and slice the remaining avocado.

Season the soup to taste with salt and pepper. Ladle into bowls and garnish with additional cilantro, avocado slices, and lemon slices.

Topopo Salad

MAKES 1 SALAD

I've heard different stories explaining why Tucson's most iconic salad is made to look like a volcano. One origin theory is that Tucson is surrounded by mountains, the most recognizable, Sentinel Peak, also known as "A" Mountain, which is often mistaken for a small volcano. It's not. But it was formed out of the lava from a volcano that erupted near there 25 million years ago and hardened into black, volcanic rock. In fact, the name Tucson translates into "at the foot of the black mountain." For this showstopper salad, you will need a 4-inch-diameter funnel with at least a 2-cup capacity, and a large serving plate with a diameter at least 4 inches bigger than the funnel.

2 cups finely chopped iceberg and/or romaine lettuce

½ cup frozen mixed vegetables (corn, carrots, green beans, peas), thawed in a colander under warm running water

1 to 2 tablespoons prepared vinaigrette salad dressing

1 corn tostada shell

¼ cup Refried Beans (page 60), warmed

4 thin jicama sticks, cut into 2- to 3-inch strips

1 tablespoon lemon or lime juice

1 tablespoon Pico de Gallo seasoning

4 small carrots or carrot sticks

6 large cooked shrimp

¼ cup finely shredded yellow cheddar cheese

1 slice tomato

1 pimiento-stuffed green olive, halved horizontally

Red or green salsa for serving

Combine the lettuce, mixed vegetables, and salad dressing in a large mixing bowl. The lettuce should be well coated, but not dripping.

Spread the inside of the tostada shell with the warm beans. Set aside, within reach.

Holding the funnel in your nondominant hand so that the wide end is facing up, fill the funnel with the lettuce mixture and press it down firmly with a spatula. Hold the hole end of the funnel while filling, then take your finger off the hole and let any extra dressing drain out into the sink.

Flip the tostada shell over onto the funnel so that the refried beans are touching the lettuce. Flip the serving plate over and place it centered on top of the tostada in the funnel. Then, flip the whole thing over and gently place it on the countertop. Carefully remove the funnel to reveal the volcano-shaped molded salad.

Dip one end of the jicama sticks in lemon or lime juice and then dip them into the Pico de Gallo seasoning. Lean the jicama sticks, vertically at even intervals, around the perimeter of the salad (chile side up), followed by the carrots and shrimp. Sprinkle the top of the salad with cheddar cheese to resemble lava. Crown your topopo with a slice of tomato and half of the pimiento-stuffed olive. While eating, once you topple your topopo, mix in some salsa for an extra kick.

Mix Salad

The taco shop closest to my house used to have a white piece of paper taped to the bottom of their menu that said "Mix Salad" across the top with a handwritten description underneath like what I've recreated in the recipe below. Eventually, the paper was taken down, but if I ask, they will still make a mix salad for me. It's a fantastic way to use up leftover carne asada. There is something so satisfying about the combo of warm meat on top of a cold salad. I love how the meat melts the cheese slightly without over-wilting the greens.

FOR THE DRESSING

¼ cup Penca's Green Tomatillo Salsa (page 47)

¼ cup balsamic vinegar

Sea salt and freshly ground black pepper to taste

½ cup extra-virgin olive oil

FOR THE SALAD

8 cups chopped romaine or iceberg lettuce

8 cups shredded red and/or green cabbage

1 cup diced cucumber

1 cup diced tomato

2 small avocados, peeled and sliced

1 cup pickled red onion (page 49, optional)

2 cups pinto beans (canned is fine), drained and rinsed

2 cups diced Carne Asada (page 115), warmed

1 cup shredded white Mexican cheese blend

Limes wedges for serving

To make the dressing, in a small bowl, whisk together the salsa, vinegar, salt, and pepper. While whisking, slowly add the oil until emulsified. Set aside.

To make the salad, in a large bowl, toss together the lettuce and cabbage, then place onto a large rimmed plate or bowl. Surround the lettuce with cucumber, tomato, avocado, and pickled red onion. Spoon the beans on top, followed by the carne asada and cheese. Pour on the dressing, squeeze on some lime juice, mix it all together, and enjoy!

Nopalitos Chopped Salad

MAKES 1 MAIN-DISH SERVING OR 2 SIDE-DISH SERVINGS

Nopalitos are an excellent example of how people adapt to their environment and get creative with the indigenous plants that surround them. Conceptually, nopalitos, which are made from the pads of the prickly pear cactus, are a little scary to eat at first. When I first picked up a package of fresh nopal pads at my local market, I examined them closely and declared them free of the pesky needles that are all over the prickly pear cactus growing all over my front yard. If you can't find fresh nopals locally, don't fret! The diced and cooked version of nopalitos are available in jars at most specialty markets and online.

1 cup jarred nopalitos, rinsed (or chopped Fresh Cactus Nopalitos—see sidebar)

1 head romaine lettuce, finely chopped (about 2 cups)

3 small tomatoes, preferably Campari, coarsely chopped (about 1 cup)

1 cup chopped cucumber

2 tablespoons chopped fresh cilantro

1 green onion, diced (about 2 tablespoons)

¼ cup thinly sliced red onion

2 tablespoons olive oil

1 tablespoon white vinegar

Juice from 2 medium-size limes

1 teaspoon dried Mexican oregano

1 small serrano chile, finely diced (optional)

Sea salt and freshly ground black pepper to taste

2 radishes, sliced

1 small avocado, peeled and diced

¼ cup crumbled Cotija or feta cheese

In a large bowl, toss nopalitos, romaine, tomatoes, cucumber, cilantro, green onion, red onion, olive oil, vinegar, lime juice, oregano, and serrano, if using. Season with salt and pepper to taste. Divide onto serving plates. Arrange the radishes and avocado around the edges and on top of the salads. Garnish with the crumbled cheese.

FRESH CACTUS NOPALITOS

In a nonstick pan over low heat, stir together 1 diced fresh nopal (cactus pad with the needles removed) with a sprig of cilantro and a pinch or two of salt. The pieces will start to release a slimy substance, but don't worry; it will absorb as the nopal pieces cook. Stir occasionally until all the liquid is absorbed, and the cactus pieces are dry looking, about 8 minutes. Remove from heat and let cool before using.

Potato Salad with Chile-Lime Vinaigrette & Red Onion

MAKES 8 SERVINGS

Sonoran food is often served garnished with pickled red onions and Mexican limes. I've incorporated those flavors into this spicy roasted potato salad. Serve it alongside one of the hot dog recipes in this book for a Sonoran-style picnic.

2 pounds small Yukon Gold potatoes, scrubbed and halved

3 tablespoons olive oil

Sonoran sea salt and freshly ground black pepper to taste

½ small red onion, minced (about ½ cup)

1 serrano chile, minced

1 tablespoon minced cilantro

2 tablespoons red wine vinegar

1 tablespoon hot sauce, such as Poblano

2 Mexican limes, 1 juiced and 1 cut into wedges

Preheat the oven to 425°F. In a large roasting pan, toss the potatoes with the olive oil. Season generously with salt and pepper. Arrange the potatoes skin-side up in a single layer. Cover pan tightly with aluminum foil; bake for 20 minutes. Remove the foil and continue roasting uncovered until the sides of the potatoes touching pan are golden brown, about 15 minutes more.

Transfer the potatoes to a mixing bowl. While they are still hot, gently toss with the red onion, serrano, cilantro, vinegar, hot sauce, and lime juice. The sauce will sink into the skin of the warm potatoes. Refrigerate until the potatoes are cool, about 30 minutes.

To serve, sprinkle with additional sea salt and garnish with the lime wedges.

Spicy Thai-Mex Slaw

Inspired by my very favorite Thai dish, Som Tum (green papaya salad), this crunchy, salty, and spicy coleslaw is an excellent companion to traditional Sonoran dishes. Serve it alongside burros and enchiladas or layered in a sandwich like the Pork Torta (page 125). The Thai fish sauce gives this slaw a burst of umami flavor, but you could always just use a bit more salt instead.

2 cups shredded green cabbage, or 1 (16-ounce) bag (about 2 cups) shredded cabbage or coleslaw blend

¼ cup minced cilantro leaves

2 green onions, thinly sliced (optional)

2 tablespoons extra-virgin olive oil

Juice from 3 Mexican limes, about 3 tablespoons

1 serrano chile, minced

A few dashes of Thai fish sauce (optional)

Sea salt and freshly ground black pepper to taste

Put the cabbage, cilantro, and green onions, if using, in a large bowl and toss together. In a small bowl, whisk together the olive oil, lime juice, chile, and fish sauce, if using, to make a dressing. Pour the dressing over the cabbage mixture and toss well. Season with salt and pepper and toss again. Let stand for at least 30 minutes to let the flavors meld before serving.

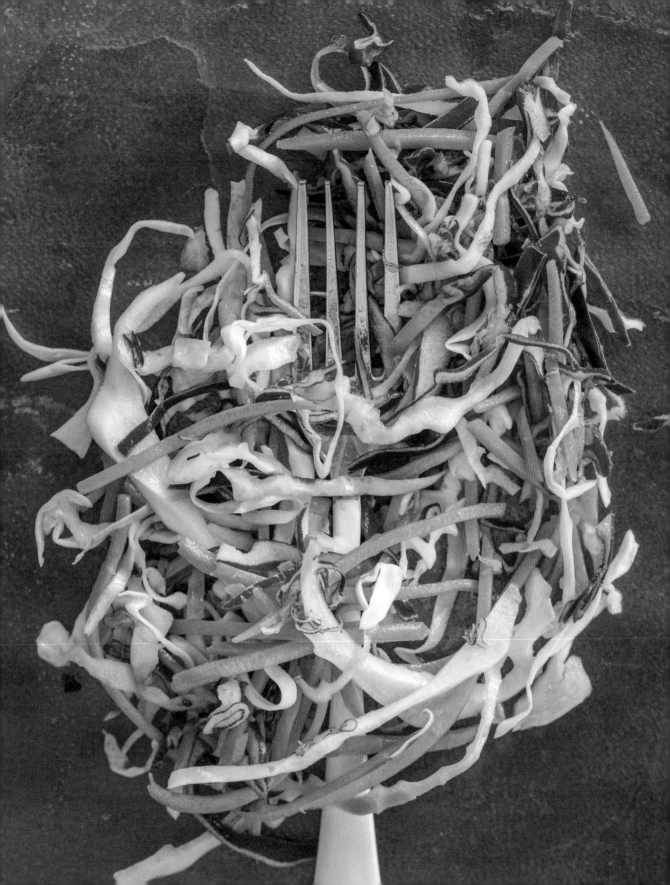

Main Dishes

For decades, ranching was the most important industry in Sonora, and beef, more than pork, was a major component of the local diet. Cowboy culture is still part of the local lore and a giant cowboy steak is a central component to a lot of people's Southwestern fantasy, with no trip to the region being complete without the iconic steak dinner, complete with thick slabs of white bread, beans, and the obligatory green salad.

Pigs were brought to this region by the Spanish. Though I have never seen one, apparently there are wild pigs (domesticated pigs that have been let loose and gone feral) all over central Arizona. These are different than Javelina, which look like wild boar but are instead a type of super-size hooved beast from the peccary family. Those I have seen. They are pack animals who arrive in my yard like an adorable family street gang, knocking over my garbage cans and eating whatever they choose to claim as their own.

Chickens are not native to the Americas, and since they can't fly very far, they had to be transported here from somewhere else. It is thought that they probably were brought to the Americas by the Polynesians before Columbus arrived. If that is true, they are immigrants who arrived here way before the Europeans did.

The Sea of Cortez is in the Mexican state of Sonora, only four to six hours away from Tucson by car. As a result, Mexican seafood restaurants are abundant here. Some of the more common seafood used in the local cuisine include shrimp, calamari (squid), marlin, and firm white fish such as cod.

Rice, beans, wheat, and corn are four of the basic defining elements of this regional cuisine, and vegetarian food is extremely common in Tucson. Sonoran-style cuisine lends itself to vegetarian variations. Meat is easily replaced with beans, eggs, and/or cheese, or one of the many varieties of vegetarian and vegan meat alternatives on the market, so it's easy to keep meat out of the picture and still feel satisfied. Many people are surprised to learn that one of the defining attributes of Sonoran food is how light and healthy it often is. One of the reasons for this is that it's common for recipes to feature an abundance of fresh produce.

Carne Asada Tacos

MAKES 8 TACOS

Carne asada translates to "grilled steak." Thin cuts of beef are cooked over a mesquite fire and served as a main dish, or chopped and used in burros, salads, and many other Sonoran-style dishes. Benjamin Galaz doesn't remember exactly when he noticed the old man selling tacos out of a cart by the freeway, just that it was the early 1990s. Even though the man and his cart vanished after just a few months, Galaz never forgot. He was inspired! He built his own food cart and soon began selling his now-famous mesquite-grilled carne asada. His business thrived, and his BK restaurants flourish. Sonoran-style carne asada has some key features: It is not marinated. It is cooked over mesquite wood. It is flavored with Sonoran sea salt (see page 19). The wood needs to be really dry. The grill, very hot. Pineapple juice is Ben's secret ingredient. It helps caramelize and tenderize the meat.

Mesquite wood or mesquite charcoal

Asada Seasoning Blend (page 28)

1 pound ½-inch skirt steaks or bottom round steaks

Squirt bottle filled with pineapple juice

8 (6-inch) flour tortillas or Corn Tortillas (page 34), warmed

2 cups Chunky Guacamole (page 42)

2 cups chopped or shredded green cabbage

1 cup pickled red onions (page 49)

1 cup Pico de Gallo Salsa (page 46)

Chiltepin Salsa (page 45) to taste

A few sliced radishes

1 cup crumbled Cotija cheese

Prepare a charcoal grill, burning the mesquite until the coal is red-hot. Season your steak(s) generously on both sides with the asada seasoning blend. Sear the steak on one side for about a minute—you want to flip the steak before you start to see the juice on the surface of the meat. Sear the meat on the other side for another minute. Squirt about a tablespoon of pineapple juice on the steak, flip it, and repeat on the other side. Flip the steak again to caramelize the meat.

Let steak rest for a minute or two, then slice the meat against the grain. Dice the meat into ¼- to ½-inch pieces. Keep warm.

To make each taco, layer the ingredients on each tortilla: Start with guacamole, then add the carne asada, cabbage, pickled onions, salsas, radishes, and cheese. Fold and eat.

COWBOY STEAKS

Making authentic cowboy steaks is easy if you have a very hot fire. When I asked Bryan Keith, the grill master at Pinnacle Peak Steakhouse, if he had any tips, he said, "Just put some love in it!" Here's a simple formula: Prepare a charcoal grill, burning mesquite wood or charcoal, until red-hot. Generously season one 20-ounce T-bone steak with garlic salt (leave on all the fat for flavor). Grill the steak 6 to 8 inches from the coals for 3 to 5 minutes per side for medium-rare. Let rest 5 to 10 minutes before serving. (See image on page 112.)

Carne Seca Enchiladas with Green Sauce

MAKES 8 ENCHILADAS

Carne seca is made by panfrying shredded beef jerky (carne seca means "dried beef") with green chiles, onions, and tomatoes. When cooked, the meat takes on more moisture, giving it a chewy texture. It takes a little while to shred the beef by hand, but it's worth the effort. If you prefer, pre-shredded dried beef is also available online and in specialty markets. In Tucson, carne seca is commonly served as a filling for burritos or scrambled with eggs for breakfast. In this recipe, it's used in savory enchiladas in a tangy green sauce. Enchiladas, like many of the dishes in this book, are easy to mix and match. You can use this recipe as a starting point. Try substituting chicken, pork, or seafood for the carne seca; red enchilada sauce for green; and yellow cheese for white, if you wish.

FOR THE CARNE SECA

2 tablespoons olive oil

2 cups finely shredded Beef Jerky (page 36) or purchased shredded dried beef

½ cup diced Anaheim, New Mexico, or Hatch green chiles

½ cup diced white onion

½ cup diced tomato

8 Corn Tortillas (page 34), warmed

2 cups Green Enchilada Sauce (page 50), warmed

1 cup shredded white cheese, such as Manchego or queso quesadilla

To make the carne seca, heat the oil in large skillet over medium heat. Add the shredded beef, green chiles, onion, and tomato. Sauté, stirring occasionally, until browned, about 10 minutes.

To make the enchiladas, preheat the broiler. Place a tortilla in the middle of an oven-safe plate. Spoon ¼ cup of the carne seca down the middle of the tortilla. Roll a parallel side of the tortilla over the meat so that the seams are on the bottom. Repeat until you have the desired serving size on the plate, usually 1, 2, or 3 enchiladas.

Spoon ¼ cup of the enchilada sauce over each rolled tortilla (so for 2 enchiladas you will need ½ cup sauce). Sprinkle the cheese over the top, then place the plate under the broiler and cook until the cheese is melted, brown, and bubbly, about 3 to 5 minutes. Watch them carefully so they don't burn. The plate will be hot, so serve doubled with another cool plate underneath to make sure that the table, and your hands, don't get burned.

The Burrito Family

The burrito is a widely known Mexican dish throughout the country, but in Tucson, it has a whole family tree with its own special branches. Here are some of the ones you will find on restaurant menus in the Tucson area.

BURROS A typical dish from the Mexican state of Sonora consisting of a large flour tortilla wrapped around a savory filling like meat, beans, or cheese.

BURRITOS Little burros. They are called that because ranchers used to carry the wraps in the saddlebags of the burros (donkeys) they were riding.

CHIMICHANGAS (CHIMIS) Fried burritos or burros, depending on their size. I would not recommend frying anything larger than a mini chimi at home. Deep-frying large objects is a task best left to a professional. Anything that you can put in a burro can be made into a chimi or a mini chimi.

ENCHILADA-STYLE A burrito, burro, or chimi smothered with warmed red or green enchilada sauce and shredded cheese. It is then placed under the broiler for a minute or two until the cheese melts.

ELEGANTE-STYLE A burrito, burro, or chimi enchilada-style with guacamole, sour cream, and pico de gallo salsa spooned over the top.

BURRITO MELT A burrito, burro, or chimi enchilada style without the enchilada sauce.

For the record, my favorite way to eat a burrito or burro is smothered in red or green enchilada sauce, sprinkled generously with cheese, and baked until the cheese is melted and the ends of the burro/burrito are nice and crispy. You can top it in a traditional style with crema and/or guacamole, though personally, I'm partial to gobs of plain Greek yogurt.

Mini Chimichangas

SERVINGS VARY

Here is an introduction to the art of deep-frying tiny burritos, from Carlotta Flores, proprietor of El Charro Café, the oldest family-owned Mexican restaurant in the United States. Her great-grand-aunt Monica Flin is widely believed to have invented the chimichanga in the late 1950s. Use one of the filling suggestions below—try mixing and matching them—or use your imagination and come up with your own. Serve savory chimis with bowls of salsa, sour cream, and guacamole for dipping. Dust sweet chimis with powdered sugar after frying.

Vegetable oil
1 (6-inch) flour tortilla for each mini chimi
About 2 tablespoons filling of choice (see below) for each mini chimi

SAVORY FILLINGS

Refried Beans (page 60) and cheese
Chopped green chiles and cheese
Chile Colorado Beef (page 122)
Shredded chicken
Shrimp with Creamy Goat Cheese–Poblano Sauce (page 141)
Carne Seca (page 116)

SWEET FILLINGS

Pie filling (apple, pumpkin, cherry, etc.)
Nutella
Peanut butter and jam

Toothpicks

Fill a large stockpot or Dutch oven with 2 inches of oil, being sure to leave at least 4 inches of clearance between the oil and the top of the pot (for safety). Set the pot over medium-high heat until the oil reads 350°F on a deep-frying thermometer.

Lay a tortilla flat on a smooth work surface. Fold up the bottom third of the tortilla to make a flat end.

Place about 2 tablespoons of the filling of your choice on the flat-end base. Then, Carlotta says: "Roll the base and filling one turn up so that the fold is in the center/widest part of the tortilla. Next, fold the two shorter ends in and roll again, once or twice until you have a neat little package."

Secure the ends with toothpicks. Repeat with the remaining tortillas and filling. Using tongs, gently place the mini chimis in the hot oil. Fry until golden, about 5 minutes, turning them as needed to brown evenly. Let drain on paper towels, then remove toothpicks and serve immediately.

VARIATION: BAKED MINI CHIMIS

Have a fear of frying? Bake the chimichangas instead at 350°F until golden brown and puffy, 12 to 15 minutes.

Chile Colorado Beef over Sonoran-Style Enchiladas

MAKES 8 TO 10 ENCHILADAS

Colorado means "red" in Spanish, and this dish is indeed a deep, vivid red.
Cubed beef simmered in red chile sauce is a popular filling for burritos around these
parts, while flat Sonoran-style enchiladas, unique to this region, are small, corn masa
pancakes covered in red enchilada sauce. I've combined the two in this unique dish.

FOR THE CHILE COLORADO

1 (14-ounce) container frozen
   red chile puree, or 2 cups Red
   Enchilada Sauce (page 50)

2 tablespoons olive oil

1½ pounds beef chuck, cut into
   1-inch pieces

4 garlic cloves, minced

3 tablespoons all-purpose or
   almond flour

1 tablespoon dried Mexican
   oregano

½ teaspoon sea salt

1 tablespoon red wine vinegar

1 teaspoon Worcestershire sauce

⅛ teaspoon adobo seasoning
   (optional)

FOR THE MASA PANCAKES

1 small potato (about 3 ounces),
   preferably Yukon Gold

2 cups masa harina, preferably
   Masienda, prepared according
   to package directions

½ teaspoon sea salt

¼ teaspoon baking soda

½ cup shredded cheddar or
   Mexican-blend cheese

2 tablespoons unsalted butter

1 tablespoon olive oil

FOR SERVING

2 cups shredded queso fresco or
   other white Mexican cheese

½ cup chopped green onions

¼ cup sliced green olives

¼ cup sliced radishes

To make the chile colorado, run the container of chile puree, if using, under hot water to thaw it slightly. Meanwhile, heat the olive oil in a large saucepan over medium heat. Remove the partially frozen disc of chile puree from its container and place it on one side of the pan. (It will thaw and cook while the beef is browning.) Add the cubed beef to the other side of the pan and sauté for 10 minutes or until cooked through; meanwhile, the chile puree should be completely liquefied. Reduce the heat to medium-low, and stir in the garlic, flour, oregano, salt, vinegar, Worcestershire sauce, and adobo seasoning until smooth. Cover the pan and simmer until thickened, 15 to 20 minutes. Keep warm.

To make the masa pancakes, peel the potato, poke it several times with a fork, and microwave until soft, 3 minutes. Let cool.

Put the prepared masa in a bowl and mix in the salt and baking soda. Smash the potato and knead into the masa mixture until smooth. Form the masa mixture into 8 to 10 balls the size of a medium egg. Place 1 ball between two pieces of wax paper. Using a rolling pin, flatten the ball into a ¼-inch-thick disk. Repeat with the remaining balls.

Heat the butter and the oil in a heavy skillet over medium heat. Fry the pancakes until golden brown, about 5 minutes on each side. Drain on paper towels.

When ready to serve, place one or two masa pancakes on each serving plate and spoon some of the warmed Chile Colorado over the top. Sprinkle with the cheese, green onions, and a few green olives and radish slices, and serve.

Adobo Pulled Pork

MAKES 10 TO 12 SERVINGS

Travis Peters is one of several chefs who represent Tucson in UNESCO City of Gastronomy events around the world. His restaurant, The Parish, features Southern cuisine with a Sonoran accent. This recipe is a three-step process: seasoning; smoking (optional), which gives it a deep flavor; and braising, which renders it meltingly tender.

5 pounds boneless pork shoulder or pork butt

¼ cup olive oil

1¼ cups Adobo Spice Rub (page 29), divided

8 cups chicken stock

3 (12-ounce) cans beer

3 cups apple cider vinegar

Juice from 3 Persian limes

1 yellow onion, roughly chopped

4 garlic cloves, peeled

1 cup (firmly packed) cilantro

1 to 2 small jalapeño chiles, roughly chopped

¼ teaspoon liquid smoke (if you skipped the smoking step)

Pat the pork dry. Rub it with the olive oil, then with ¾ cup of the adobo spice rub, forming a paste all over the meat. Cover with plastic wrap and refrigerate for 24 to 48 hours.

If you are smoking the pork, fill a smoker with mesquite and preheat it to 180°F to 220°F. Place the seasoned pork as far from the fire as possible. Cover and smoke the pork for 6 hours, rotating the pork, rearranging the coals, and adding wood as needed every hour to keep a lively plume of smoke going. (If you are making this ahead, you can cool the pork at this point and refrigerate the meat for up to 3 days before braising.)

Preheat the oven to 225°F. In a large saucepan, bring the stock, beer, vinegar, and lime juice to a boil over high heat. In a blender or food processor, puree the onion, garlic, cilantro, jalapeño, remaining ½ cup adobo spice rub, and liquid smoke, if using, until smooth. Place the smoked pork in a deep roasting pan and evenly distribute the puréed mixture over the top and sides. Add the boiling broth mixture, leaving the top inch of the pork uncovered. Cover the roasting pan with foil. Braise in the oven until tender, about 12 hours.

Transfer the pork to a cutting board. Pour the braising liquid into a large pot and boil until reduced by half, about 20 minutes. Meanwhile, shred the warm pork with two large forks. Add the shredded pork to the reduced liquid and let cool. Refrigerate overnight, then skim off the fat.

When ready to use, rewarm the pork before serving.

VARIATION: PORK TORTA

Warm ½ to 1 cup pulled pork on a hot skillet until crispy. Spread 2 tablespoons warmed Refried Beans (page 60) on one half of a toasted bolillo or French roll. Layer on the warm pork, ¼ cup Spicy Thai-Mex Slaw (page 108), 2 to 4 slices avocado, and several cilantro leaves. Spread the other roll half with mayonnaise and, if desired, barbecue sauce. Place on top of the layered half and serve immediately. Makes 1 sandwich.

Seis Kitchen's Chicken Taquitos

MAKES 16 TAQUITOS

Taquitos translates to "little tacos." The fillings are minimal, usually just a bit of meat or cheese rolled inside a corn tortilla and then baked or fried so that they have a satisfying crunch. Condiments can be spooned over the top or served on the side for dipping. Seis Kitchen's extremely popular version has become a must-try dish on Tucson's best-of lists. Erika Muñoz, the co-proprietor of the restaurant, is also a trained nutritionist who says that flash-frying helps make her taquitos healthier. Her technique keeps the chicken moist on the inside and crispy on the outside. Serve with a side of Calabacitas (page 67).

FOR THE POACHED CHICKEN

1 carrot
1 celery stalk
1 small red onion
1 garlic clove, peeled
2 tablespoons red chile powder
1 tablespoon dried
  Mediterranean oregano
1 teaspoon sea salt
1 teaspoon freshly ground
  black pepper
1½ quarts water
1 pound boneless, skinless
  chicken thighs

FOR THE TAQUITOS

Canola oil, for frying
16 corn tortillas
Toothpicks

FOR SERVING

¼ cup sour cream or Mexican
  crema mixed with your favorite
  hot sauce to taste
Crumbled Cotija cheese
Chunky Guacamole (page 42)

In a large pot, combine the carrot, celery, onion, garlic clove, chile powder, oregano, salt, pepper, and water and bring to a boil over high heat. Reduce the heat to low and add the chicken. Simmer the chicken until it falls apart easily, about 1½ hours.

Using a slotted spoon, remove the chicken from the poaching liquid and shred with two forks. Place the shredded chicken in a bowl and add enough of the poaching liquid to keep the meat moist but not submerged (about 1 cup). Keep warm. Discard the remaining poaching liquid.

To make the taquitos, fill a large Dutch oven with 2 inches of oil, being sure to leave at least 4 inches of clearance between the oil and the top of the pot (for safety). Warm the oil over medium heat until it reads 375°F on a deep-frying thermometer.

While the oil is heating, place 2 to 3 tablespoons of the shredded chicken down the center of each tortilla. Roll up each tortilla firmly around the filling and secure with a toothpick. Use tongs to gently place 3 to 4 taquitos at a time into the hot oil. Fry, turning once, until the edges are light golden brown, 30 to 60 seconds. Drain on paper towels before serving. Bring the cooking oil back to 375°F between batches.

Serve warm, drizzled with the spiked sour cream and sprinkled with cilantro and Cotija. Serve with guacamole for dipping.

VARIATION: BAKED TAQUITOS
Skip the frying step. Instead, brush or spray the filled taquitos with a little olive oil and cook them seam side down on a parchment-lined baking sheet in a 375°F oven until brown and crispy, about 8 minutes.

One-Pot Arroz con Pollo

MAKES 6 TO 8 SERVINGS

When I asked locals which Tucson-centric recipes they would most like to see included in this book, quite a few people mentioned arroz con pollo, and I've always found chicken and rice to be a comforting combo. This is a great make-ahead recipe for work-day lunches. At first glance, salsa de chile fresco may look like pureed tomato sauce, but it's got a medium-spicy kick of heat that will convince you otherwise.

2 tablespoons unsalted butter

1 pound boneless, skinless chicken thighs

2 cups diced white onion

1 cup Arborio rice

½ cup good quality, spicy red wine, such as Malbec

4 cups chicken broth, divided

1 teaspoon granulated chicken-flavored bouillon, preferably Knorr brand

4 cloves garlic, minced

1 (8-ounce) can salsa de chile fresco, preferably El Pato brand

1 tablespoon red wine vinegar

1 cup frozen peas and carrots

1 tablespoon red chile powder

1 tablespoon dried Mexican oregano

⅛ teaspoon cayenne pepper

½ cup crumbled Cotija cheese, plus more for serving

Sea salt and freshly ground black pepper to taste

In a large, heavy-bottomed skillet or Dutch oven, melt 1 tablespoon of the butter over medium-high heat. Add the chicken thighs and onion and cook until the chicken is browned, about 4 minutes on each side. The onion will soften. Remove the chicken, leaving the onion in the pan, and set aside. Add the rice and remaining 1 tablespoon of butter, then sauté until the rice is lightly browned, about 3 minutes.

Add the wine and use a wooden spoon to dislodge the brown bits stuck to the bottom of the pan. Add 2 cups of the broth, the chicken-flavored bouillon, and the garlic. Simmer until most of the liquid has been absorbed, about 10 minutes.

Add the salsa, vinegar, peas and carrots, chile powder, oregano, cayenne, and the remaining 2 cups broth. Stir, then return the browned chicken to the pot with its juices. Reduce the heat to medium, cover the pot, and simmer until all the liquid is absorbed, 30 to 35 minutes.

Stir in the Cotija cheese. Season to taste with salt and black pepper. Spoon the rice over the chicken pieces and serve in wide shallow bowls sprinkled with additional cheese.

Chicken or Steak Fingers Inspired by Lucky Wishbone

MAKES 4 SERVINGS

Lucky Wishbone claims to have been Tucson's first fast-food restaurant. They've been open since 1953, and people still go crazy for their fried chicken, steak, and shrimp. My favorites are their chicken and steak fingers combo, as well as the fried chicken gizzards. Thank you to The Parish chef Travis Peters for helping me figure out this copycat recipe. Serve these along with a thick slice of garlic bread, as they do at the Lucky Wishbone.

FOR THE STEAK FINGERS

2 cups all-purpose flour

1 tablespoon Lawry's Seasoned Salt

1 pound chicken tenders or thin steak strips, such as bottom round

½ cup Greek yogurt

¼ cup milk

1 large egg

Dash or two of hot sauce

FOR THE DIPPING SAUCE

½ cup prepared cocktail sauce

1 tablespoon prepared horseradish

Preheat the oven to 350°F. Line the bottom of a rimmed baking sheet fitted with a wire baking rack with foil.

Place flour and seasoned salt in a resealable plastic bag. Shake to mix. Add the chicken or steak, seal the bag, and then shake again to coat the pieces well.

In a large bowl, whisk together the yogurt, milk, egg, and hot sauce. Using tongs, transfer the coated chicken or steak pieces to the yogurt mixture and roll them around to coat well. Add the chicken or steak pieces back to the bag to coat in the flour mixture a second time. Transfer the coated pieces to the prepared baking sheet. Bake until the steak or chicken fingers are cooked through and golden brown, 20 to 25 minutes, turning them over halfway through.

To make the dipping sauce, in a small bowl, mix together the cocktail sauce and horseradish.

Serve the chicken or steak fingers warm with the spicy dipping sauce on the side.

Chicken Mole Amarillo

MAKES 4 TO 6 SERVINGS

Nuttier and less sweet than its chocolate-based cousin, this version of mole amarillo is the personal creation of Chef Suzana Davila of Tucson's Café Poca Cosa. She specializes in these complex sauces, and her recipes are longtime local favorites. Serve this dish with tortillas and a pretty salad, as Suzana would.

FOR THE MOLE

8 yellow bell peppers

4 garlic cloves, peeled

2 yellow tomatoes

2 Güero (Caribe) chiles

½ cup raw sesame seeds

1 cup raw almonds

½ cup raw pepitas (shelled pumpkin seeds), plus more for garnish

3 to 4 cups chicken broth

2 tablespoons olive oil

½ cup chopped white onion

1 teaspoon dried Mexican oregano

6 (6-inch) corn tostada shells

2 teaspoons granulated chicken-flavored bouillon, preferably Knorr brand

FOR THE CHICKEN

2 tablespoons olive oil

¼ cup chopped white onion

6 boneless, skinless chicken breasts or thighs

1 bay leaf

Sea salt

Corn tortillas, for serving

Preheat the broiler. Place the bell peppers, garlic, tomatoes, and chiles on a foil-lined rimmed baking sheet. Place in the oven and broil until the skins are blackened and charred, about 15 minutes. When cool enough to handle, remove the stems, seeds, and skins from the peppers, tomatoes, and chiles.

In a dry 12-inch skillet over medium heat, toast the sesame seeds until golden brown, about 2 minutes, stirring to keep from burning. Remove from the skillet and let cool. Toast the almonds and pepitas in the same skillet until the pepitas puff up but do not darken, about 2 minutes; remove the almonds and pepitas from the skillet and let cool. Once cooled, transfer the sesame seeds, almonds, and pepitas to a food processor or blender. Add 1 cup of the broth and blend until smooth.

Heat 1 tablespoon of olive oil in the same skillet over medium heat. Sauté the onion along with the oregano in the oil until the onion is tender but not brown, about 5 minutes. Add the pureed nut mixture and stir well. Reduce the heat to low.

Place the roasted peppers, tomatoes, chiles, and another 1 cup of the chicken broth to the food processor or blender and blend until smooth. Add it to the onion-nut mixture in the skillet.

Break the tostada shells into pieces and pulse in the food processor or blender with the roasted garlic, bouillon, and 1 cup broth. Stir into the skillet mixture. Continue to cook the mole, stirring often, over low heat for 20 to 25 minutes. If the sauce becomes too thick, add the fourth cup of broth.

While the mole is simmering, heat 2 tablespoons olive oil in another large skillet over medium heat. Sauté the ¼ cup chopped onion, the chicken, and bay leaf until chicken is cooked through, about 10 minutes.

Pour the mole over the cooked chicken and allow to simmer for an additional 10 minutes. Add salt to taste. Serve garnished with pepitas with the tortillas on the side.

Spicy Citrus Shrimp Ceviche Tostadas

MAKES 2 SERVINGS

Citrus is one of Arizona's major export crops. The cool thing about ceviche is that the acids from the citrus juice "cook" the shrimp without applying any heat. Orange essential oil can be found online or in the baking section of the market and is optional. Be sure to use only essential oils that are sold for ingestion.

1 pound medium-size raw shrimp (the freshest possible)

Juice from 2 large lemons and 1 large lime, or more if needed

4 (6-inch) corn tortillas

Olive oil cooking spray

1 clementine, tangerine, or small orange

1 cup diced cucumber

2 tablespoons diced red onion

2 tablespoons olive oil

1 serrano chile, minced

1 tablespoon chopped cilantro

2 drops orange essential oil (optional)

Sea salt and freshly ground black pepper to taste

1 avocado, diced

Hot sauce for serving

Peel and devein the shrimp, if necessary. Place the shrimp in a glass or ceramic (not metal) bowl. Add enough of the lemon and lime juice to cover the shrimp completely. Cover and refrigerate for at least 4 hours or overnight. The shrimp will be completely white inside and pink outside when they are ready.

Preheat the oven to 350°F degrees. Place the tortillas on a baking sheet; spray lightly will olive oil, then bake until crispy, flipping halfway through, about 6 minutes.

Drain the shrimp and chop it into small pieces. Return to the bowl and discard the liquid. Finely grate the clementine zest and add it to the bowl with the shrimp. Using a thin, sharp knife, remove and discard the pith and membranes from the clementine, then finely dice the segments and add them to the bowl with the shrimp along with any clementine juice. Stir in the cucumber, red onion, olive oil, chile, cilantro, and orange essential oil, if using. Season to taste with salt and pepper. Refrigerate the ceviche for at least 20 minutes and up to 4 hours to let the flavors meld.

Place 2 crisp tortillas on each of 2 plates. Using a slotted spoon, divide the ceviche among the tortillas, dividing evenly. Top with diced avocado and hot sauce. Serve immediately.

Coctel De Camarones (Sonoran-Style Shrimp Cocktail)

MAKES 2 SERVINGS

The shrimp cocktail I grew up with in Ohio was reserved for special occasions. It was served in a chilled martini glass filled with crushed ice topped with a dollop of horseradish, and lemon juice–infused ketchup, the shrimp dangling around the rim. I loved it. Mexican style shrimp cocktail is a more casual affair, but just as festive. It is most traditionally served layered in the kind of glass used for ice cream sundaes, along with the customary long spoon. This cocktail is usually made with seafood, chopped onions, and cucumber mixed with Clamato, but I like the fresher taste by mixing it with vegetable juice cocktail and my own ratio of clam juice. While shrimp cocktail is often served as an appetizer, I make it into a main by serving it with rice, beans, and tortillas and a small salad. There are many brands of hot sauce specifically made to be served with seafood in Tucson today. Castillo, Huichol, and La Guacamaya are a few of my favorites.

1 cup unsweetened Bloody Mary mix (I like Trader Joe's version) or tomato vegetable juice cocktail such as V8 Spicy Hot

¼ cup bottled clam juice

2 tablespoons fresh lime juice

¼ cup chopped cucumber

2 tablespoons chopped white or red onion

1 tablespoon chopped fresh cilantro

½ pound medium-size peeled and cooked shrimp

½ avocado, roughly chopped

Mexican hot sauce for seafood (see note) to taste

Mexican lime wedges for garnish

In a liquid measuring cup, stir together the Bloody Mary mix, clam juice, and lime juice.

Layer the cucumber, onion, cilantro, and shrimp into 2 sundae dishes or large glasses. Pour in the vegetable juice mixture to fill. Top with the avocado. Serve with lime wedges and Mexican seafood hot sauce.

Cod Tlalpeño in Foil Packets

MAKES 4 SERVINGS

Foil packets are a super easy, and forgiving, way to prepare fish. You can put almost any combination of vegetables in with the fish, so feel free to experiment. A quarter pound of cod will usually take about 15 to 20 minutes to cook at 400°F. If you use potatoes or root vegetables, slice them very thin. Some other ingredients to try are green olives; pico de gallo or salsa verde; minced chipotles in adobe sauce; squash, corn, kale, spinach, or other greens. My version was inspired by a popular soup originating from the Mexican village of Tlalpan, and all the ingredients are common to Sonoran cuisine as well. Chickpeas were introduced by the Spanish into the Southwest along the Rio Grande by 1630 and spread to the Santa Cruz and other waterways by 1700. Native Americans and Hispanics historically ate the beans green and dried.

½ cup boiling water

8 dried chiles de arbol

4 small lemons

4 (4-ounce) cod fillets

Olive oil

1 cup canned chickpeas, rinsed and drained

4 large garlic cloves, crushed and peeled

1 medium shallot, sliced into thin slices (about ½ cup)

1 carrot sliced into thin coins (about ½ cup)

4 small rosemary sprigs

Sea salt to taste

Preheat oven to 400°F.

Pour ½ cup boiling water over the chiles and let steep for 5 minutes to soften; drain and set aside.

Cut 2 of the lemons into thin slices. Cut four 12-by-12-inch pieces of foil and place them on a work surface. Divide the slices among the foil pieces, placing them in the center. Top with the softened chiles. Lay the cod on top of the lemon slices and chiles and drizzle with oil. Top with the chickpeas, garlic, shallot, carrot, and rosemary, dividing evenly. Cut the remaining 2 lemons in half and squeeze each half over the top of each packet. Season generously with salt.

To make each packet, pinch two long ends of the foil together and roll the foil down over the top of fish, then roll the two short sides up from the bottom to make a secure packet that will hold in all the steam. Transfer the packets to a rimmed baking sheet. Bake for 20 minutes.

Remove from the oven and let rest for 2 minutes while the packets cool slightly. The fish will continue to steam inside. The chiles will add a subtle smokiness but only a tiny bit of heat to the dish if you discard them, along with the rosemary, before eating. Serve the wrapped packets with a warning that while the foil should be cool to the touch, that hot steam may escape as the foil is unwrapped.

Shrimp with Creamy Goat Cheese–Poblano Sauce

MAKES 3 TO 4 SERVINGS

Chef Maria Mazon of BOCA Tacos y Tequila is a sauce master. Her goat cheese–poblano sauce is awesome over grilled chicken breasts, in enchiladas stuffed with mushrooms, or tossed with pasta. Here we added cooked shrimp to the sauce, then served it in deep red cabbage cups, which add a visual contrast to the white sauce and a slightly peppery taste. You can substitute soy sauce for the Maggi Jugo if necessary. Goat cheese has been a staple in Sonora for centuries. The Spanish brought both goats and cheesemaking techniques to the desert region.

2 poblano chiles
1 medium white onion, halved
12 ounces soft goat cheese
1 (12-ounce) can evaporated milk
¼ cup water
2 teaspoons garlic powder
1 teaspoon sea salt
Ground white pepper to taste
Dash of Maggi Jugo Seasoning Sauce (see page 16)
1 pound cooked medium shrimp
1 small red or green cabbage

Preheat the broiler or grill.

Remove the stems (and seeds if you want the sauce to be less spicy) from the chiles. Broil or grill the chiles and onion, turning the chiles occasionally so that the skins are blistered on all sides, about 10 minutes.

Transfer the chiles and onion to a large saucepan or Dutch oven. Add 10 ounces of the goat cheese (reserving about 2 ounces), the evaporated milk, ¼ cup water, garlic powder, salt, white pepper, and Maggi Jugo. Bring to a boil over medium-high heat. Pour into a blender and let cool for 10 minutes. Blend until smooth, then strain through a sieve. Return the mixture to the pot and simmer over low heat for 20 minutes.

Set 6 to 8 shrimp aside for garnish. Stir the rest of the shrimp into the sauce and cook over low heat until warmed through, about 5 minutes.

To make the cabbage cups, cut the cabbage head in half vertically from the stem to the crown. Cut the core out of both halves of the cabbage, then cut the halves vertically down the middle. Separate the cabbage leaves and wash them well before filling.

Fill the cabbage cups with shrimp mixture and garnish each with a shrimp piece. Crumble the remaining 2 ounces goat cheese over the top.

Classic Cheese Crisp

MAKES 2 TO 4 SERVINGS

Southern Arizona restaurants started selling this popular appetizer more than 50 years ago, and it's become a staple of our local Sonoran-style cuisine. It's like a quesadilla, except instead of folding the tortilla over it is baked open faced until the tortilla is crispy and the cheese is melted. The variations show how a few simple changes turn it into an entirely different dish—adding a sauce and savory topping to make Mexican pizza or folding over the tortilla and grilling for a classic quesadilla.

Any size flour tortilla (the bigger, the more impressive)

Shredded Mexican-blend cheese, as needed

8 to 10 strips of roasted green chile (optional)

8 to 10 cilantro leaves (optional)

FOR THE CHIPOTLE-RANCH DRIZZLE

½ cup prepared ranch dressing

2 teaspoons adobo sauce from a jar of chipotle chiles in adobo

Preheat the oven to 350°F. Place the tortilla flat on a pizza pan or baking sheet. Poke the tortilla all over with a small, pointy knife to prevent puffing in the oven. Bake for 5 minutes.

Remove the tortilla from the oven and cover it generously with cheese. Arrange the chile strips, if using, on top, then bake again until the cheese is melted, another 3 to 5 minutes.

To make the chipotle-ranch drizzle, in a small bowl, mix the ranch dressing with the adobo sauce until blended. Transfer to a squeeze bottle.

Garnish the cheese crisp with cilantro leaves, if using, and squeeze the chipotle-ranch drizzle in a spiral pattern over the top. Cut the tortilla into wedges with a pizza cutter or long knife and serve hot.

VARIATION: MEXICAN PIZZA
Follow the directions above but spread a thin layer of Green or Red Enchilada Sauce (page 50) on the baked tortilla before you add the cheese. Bake again as directed above, then top with chopped black olives and green onions when it comes out of the oven.

VARIATION: QUESADILLA
Skip the initial baking step. Cover half of the flour tortilla with cheese followed by an optional layer of roasted chopped green chiles. Fold the other tortilla half over the cheese to form a half-moon shape. Bake at 350°F until the cheese melts, about 3 minutes. Slice with a pizza cutter and serve.

"Taco Night" Hard-Shell Tacos

MAKES 4 SERVINGS

Crunchy taco shells that came in a box; McCormick Taco Seasoning that came in a little pouch; ground beef; the obligatory lettuce; and a shake of Parmesan cheese from a green can; that was taco night in the '70s at my house. My crunchy taco game has evolved somewhat over the years, but its roots remain intact. Crunchy taco shells now come in amazing flavors, and McCormick Taco Seasoning is still tasty, especially the hot version. I found taco seasoning works just as well mixed with whole beans as it does ground beef, and Parmesan cheese is still a decent substitution for Cotija, but skip the green can please... and do pile on the veggies. These tacos taste like home to me. My home in Tucson.

2 (14.5-ounce) cans pinto beans, drained and rinsed

½ cup water

1 packet taco seasoning, preferably McCormick's Hot, or Jackie's "Taco" Seasoning Blend (page 28)

1 box of taco shells, preferably Old El Paso's Bold Spicy Cheddar Stand'N Stuff

4 cups chopped romaine lettuce

1 cup chopped tomatoes

1 cup chopped red onion

½ cup good-quality shredded or grated Parmesan cheese

Bottled Italian salad dressing (I like Newman's Garlic and Parmesan)

Taco sauce to taste

Lemon wedges for serving

Heat the beans, ½ cup water, and taco seasoning in a medium saucepan over medium heat, stirring until well combined and warmed through, about 5 minutes.

Heat the taco shells according to package directions, then transfer to a platter.

Put the lettuce, tomatoes, red onion, cheese, salad dressing, taco sauce, and lemon wedges in bowls or leave them in the bottles they came in and set them on the table or countertop, so everyone can add as much as they want. Transfer the warm beans to a bowl and let everyone construct their own tacos. I start with beans at the bottom, then taco sauce, cheese, lettuce, tomato, onion, a splash of Italian dressing, more cheese, more taco sauce, and a squeeze of lemon over everything.

If your tacos start to fall over, anchor them with a handful of romaine lettuce on either side to hold them upright.

Modern Chiles Rellenos

MAKES 2 SERVINGS

Cheese-stuffed chiles are a classic local combo, and chiles, be it the meal-sized meaty poblano relleno, the ever popular jalapeño popper, or the small grilled yellow peppers served alongside entrees at restaurants, are finally taking center stage and shining after being buried under a heavy, fried batter for decades. If you can't find queso fresco, you can use a shredded Mexican-cheese blend instead. For a smokier flavor, I leave the charred skin of the chiles intact after broiling.

4 poblano chiles

2 large eggs, beaten

1 cup shredded Manchego, Oaxaca, queso quesadilla, and/or Asadero cheese

¼ cup cream cheese, softened

1 cup panko bread crumbs

1 tablespoon unsalted butter, melted

1 cup Green Enchilada Sauce (page 50), warmed

Preheat the broiler. Lay the chiles on a flat surface so that they lay flat vertically with the stems pointing away from you. Cut an oval-shaped hole out of the top of each chile, leaving a deep well and the stems intact. Remove the pith and seeds. Place hollowed chiles, opening side down, in a metal or ceramic baking dish. Broil until the skins start to char and bubble; flip the chiles and char on the other side. Remove the chiles from the oven and let cool. Reduce the oven heat to 400°F.

Mince the ovals that were cut from the poblano chiles. In a small bowl, mix together the eggs, cheeses, and ½ cup of the panko. Stir in the minced chile. Spoon the cheese mixture into the center of the chiles, dividing evenly, and place them back in the baking dish, opening-side up. In another small bowl, stir together the remaining ½ cup panko and the melted butter, then sprinkle evenly over the exposed cheese mixture in the chiles. Bake until the filling is heated through and the panko is golden, about 10 minutes.

To serve, divide the chile rellenos among 2 shallow bowls or rimmed plates, 2 per serving, and top with the warm sauce.

Three-Sisters Power Bowl

MAKES 4 SERVINGS

Corn, beans, and squash are three of the earliest domesticated crops grown
by Native Americans in the Sonoran region. Nicknamed the "Three Sisters," they
thrive when planted close together, and when eaten together they are nutritionally
complete. Let the power of these three sisters fuel your day! If you've never tried
tepary beans, this recipe, which was inspired by these native ingredients,
is an excellent place to start. They have a rich, meaty flavor and firm texture.
They're available online, but you can substitute other prepared beans instead.
To quickly thaw the corn, place it in a colander under cold running water.

3 cups vegetable or chicken broth

1 cup Penca's Green Tomatillo Salsa (page 47)

2 cups uncooked quinoa

1 tablespoon chia seeds

¼ cup chopped cilantro

1 cup zucchini or summer squash, diced or spiralized

1 tablespoon unsalted butter

4 eggs

Sea salt and freshly ground black pepper to taste

2 cups tepary beans, prepared according to package directions

1 cup frozen roasted corn kernels, thawed

2 large ripe avocados, sliced

½ cup Pico de Gallo Salsa (page 46)

Bring the broth and green tomatillo salsa to a boil in a medium pot. Add the quinoa, reduce the heat to medium-low, cover, and simmer for 12 minutes, or according to package directions. Remove from the heat, stir in the chia seeds and cilantro, add the zucchini, cover, and let steam for 5 minutes.

Meanwhile, heat the butter in a large nonstick skillet over medium heat. Fry the eggs to your desired doneness. Season with salt and pepper.

Divide the prepared quinoa among 4 serving bowls. Arrange the prepared beans, corn, zucchini, avocado slices, and chunky pico de gallo salsa around each bowl and top each with an egg. Serve warm.

Street Snacks at Home

Snacking in Tucson is an art unto itself. There are food trucks and little shops all over town that sell only frozen treats and culturally unique Mexican street snacks.

These street snacks were born from the fine art of improvisation probably mixed with a little late-night desperation. The skilled snack chef has learned to look at where they are, be it in the middle of a mini-mart or standing in the yellow glow of the open refrigerator late at night, and say, "Yes! I will take these random ingredients that sit before me, and then make something fabulous!" For the skilled snack chef knows there are no mistakes, only opportunities.

Sonoran-Style Hot Dogs

MAKES 4 HOT DOGS

Daniel Contreras of El Guero Canelo was presented with a James Beard America's Classics Award for the Sonoran-style hot dog. He calls his bacon-wrapped hot dogs in bolillo rolls with a smear of pinto beans and topped with onions, tomatoes, and chiles, "weenies." He specified that you can use any kind of hot dog, be it pork, beef, chicken, or plant-based—and the same goes for the bacon.

FOR THE JALAPEÑO SAUCE
6 jalapeño chiles

FOR THE HOT DOGS
4 traditionally sized hot dogs
4 long strips uncooked bacon
4 grilled yellow Güero (Caribe) chiles
4 bolillo rolls
½ cup pinto beans, warmed, drained of liquid
½ cup diced white onion, sautéed in 2 tablespoons butter until soft
½ cup diced tomatoes
Yellow mustard, in a squeeze bottle if possible
Mayonnaise, in a squeeze bottle if possible

To make the jalapeño sauce, wash and remove stems and seeds from the jalapeños. Put them in a blender or food processor and process until smooth. Use a rubber spatula to scrape into a plastic squeeze bottle or bowl and refrigerate until ready to use.

Preheat the grill or heat a griddle or cast iron pan over medium heat. Wrap each hot dog in a strip of bacon. Cook the bacon-wrapped hot dogs, starting with the loose ends of the bacon touching the grate, griddle, or pan to seal it to the hot dog. Using tongs, turn the hot dog frequently so that it browns evenly on all sides, about 3 to 5 minutes. Remove from heat, then grill the chiles on the same skillet, turning once until browned and slightly soft, about 3 minutes.

Turn each roll on its side and split it down its length with a small sharp knife. Put one cooked hot dog into each bun. For each bun, spoon in 2 tablespoons each of the beans, sautéed onions, and diced tomatoes. Then squirt on about a teaspoon each of the yellow mustard, mayonnaise, and jalapeño sauce.

Serve with the grilled yellow Güero chile on the side. I recommend biting off the end of the chile and then squeezing the juice out on top of the hot dog.

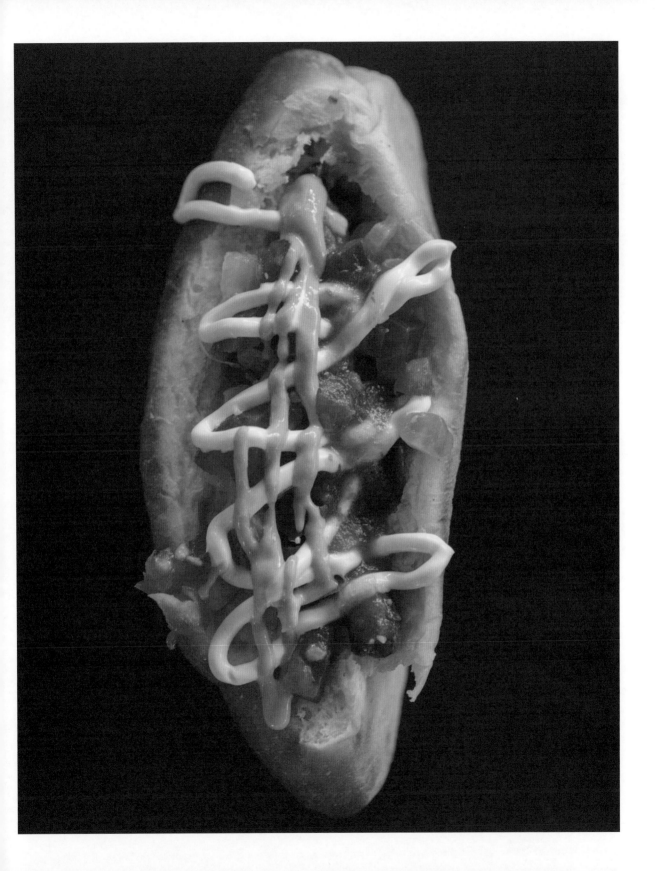

Beanie Weenie Tacos

MAKES 4 TACOS

This taco was inspired by one of my favorite after-school snacks as a kid: sliced hot dogs and canned baked beans. Now I eat them in taco form! These hot dogs are a lot less sweet than Beanie Weenies though, because I use charro beans instead of canned baked beans. Use natural casing hot dogs, if possible. I split them in half after boiling so they are crisp. Use flour tortillas for this recipe. Their chewiness is a bit more like a traditional hot dog bun than corn tortillas. BOCA Tacos Y Tequila's chef Maria Mazon has a similar hot dog taco at her restaurant, and she gave me the formula for the sauce, which is simply (yet brilliantly) equal parts ketchup, yellow mustard, mayonnaise, and white vinegar. Thanks, Maria!

FOR THE BOCA HOT DOG SAUCE
¼ cup ketchup
¼ cup yellow mustard
¼ cup mayonnaise
¼ cup white vinegar

FOR THE HOT DOGS
4 natural-casing hot dogs, such as Nathan's Famous
Water as needed
2 tablespoons olive oil
8 (6-inch) flour tortillas
1 cup prepared Charro Beans, warmed (page 59)
4 strips cooked bacon, crumbled
½ cup pickled red onions (page 49)

To make the BOCA hot dog sauce, in a bowl, mix together the ketchup, mustard, mayonnaise, and vinegar. Transfer to a plastic squeeze bottle or cover the bowl and refrigerate until ready to use.

To make the hot dogs, in a large covered nonstick sauté pan, simmer the hot dogs in ½ inch of water until the water is absorbed, about 8 minutes. Remove the hot dogs from the heat and slice them lengthwise with a paring knife. Reduce the heat to medium. Add the olive oil and heat until shimmering. Return the hot dogs to the pan and cook cut-side down until browned and crisp, about 2 minutes. Flip and cook for another minute or two on the other side.

Warm the tortillas in a dry nonstick skillet over medium heat for 30 seconds on each side, then stack two tortillas on a plate so that they overlap in the middle but are long enough to fit a hot dog. Put a hot dog on top, then spoon on ¼ cup beans, scatter on one slice of bacon, heap on ⅛ cup pickled onions, and squirt the sauce over everything. Fold and enjoy.

TostiNachos

MAKES 4 SERVINGS

This popular Mexican street snack (also called DoriNachos, TostiTacos, or TostiLocos) made its way up to Tucson by way of Mexico City, and changes names depending on what's in the bag and the type of chip you use (Tostitos or Doritos). No matter what you decide to call them, at home they're perfect for any random snack opportunity, including parties or game-day buffet tables. Simply lay out the ingredients and let everyone build their own creations. While these typically don't include meat—without it the chips stay crispy longer—feel free to add shredded chicken, carnitas, or ground beef if the spirit moves you.

2 cups prepared nacho cheese sauce, such as Rosarita

⅓ cup vegetable or chicken broth

4 small (3-ounce) bags Tostitos Salsa Verde chips

1 (10-ounce) bag steam-able frozen corn, prepared according to package directions

4 ounces sliced pickled jalapeño chiles, drained

4 ounces Cotija cheese, crumbled

Combine the nacho cheese sauce and the broth in a medium saucepan; warm, stirring occasionally, over low heat until warmed and smooth, 6 to 8 minutes.

Turn the bags on their sides and slice open lengthwise with kitchen scissors and puff the bag out a bit to make a wide base for the filling. Ladle the warm cheese sauce over the chips, then spoon in the corn and jalapeños, dividing evenly. Sprinkle with the Cotija cheese. Serve with a fork.

POUR ON THE CHEESE

Nachos made with melted cheese are what I would call American food, but like tacos and burritos they have become synonymous with Mexican food in general. Queso dip (nacho cheese sauce) was much mocked in Tucson restaurants for many years for not being Sonoran. (It's Tex-Mex.) Someone ordering queso dip in a Sonoran restaurant was often mocked by the person they were talking to in an affected Texan accent, which, frankly, wasn't very nice. And heck, queso dip is great. Is this an example of how humanity has evolved? Perhaps.

Walking Tacos

MAKES 4 SERVINGS

Walking tacos are another ingenious snack that you eat right out of the bag. They are similar to TostiNachos, but with toppings that are more common to tacos than nachos.

1 (15-ounce) can black beans, drained and rinsed

2 tablespoons water

1 tablespoon prepared taco seasoning or Jackie's "Taco" Seasoning Blend (page 28)

4 (3-ounce) bags hot sauce–flavored tortilla chips, such as Doritos Tapatio

¾ cup crumbled white Mexican cheese, such as Cotija

1 cup chopped lettuce

½ cup chopped tomatoes

½ cup Mexican crema, sour cream, or plain Greek yogurt

Salsa and/or taco sauce to taste

In a small saucepan, combine the beans, water, and taco seasoning. Cook over low heat, stirring occasionally, until warm, about 5 minutes.

Turn the chip bags on their sides and slice open lengthwise with kitchen scissors and puff the bag out a bit to make a wide base for the filling. Spoon over the beans, cheese, lettuce, tomatoes, crema, and salsa, dividing equally. Serve with a fork.

Duros with Calamari

MAKES 1 TO 2 SERVINGS

Duros are a popular Mexican snack food made from puffed wheat. This recipe is for a single, giant duro topped with calamari and veggies. Basically, it's a delicious seafood salad on top of a puffy cracker. You can buy duros either pre-puffed or as flat pellets that look like dried pasta sheets. The pellets will need to be fried in hot oil until they puff up. Pickled pig skin is sometimes served as one of the toppings. I've opted for calamari marinated in a light lemon vinaigrette instead. I'm using the milder Tajín chile-lime seasoning here instead of the more piquant Pico de Gallo seasoning.

⅓ pound fresh or frozen calamari tubes

2 Mexican limes

Sea salt to taste

Peanut or canola oil for frying (optional)

1 large rectangle-shaped duro pellet (pre-puffed or flat)

2 tablespoons Mexican crema

1 cup shredded iceberg lettuce or cabbage

¼ cup diced cucumber

¼ cup diced tomatoes

2 tablespoons diced red onion

¼ cup grated or crumbled Cotija cheese

Chamoy to taste

Chile-lime salt to taste, such as Tajín

Bring a medium pot of water to boil. Add the calamari and cook until tender, about 1 minute. Drain, then rinse under cold water, and drain again. Transfer to a medium bowl. Squeeze the juice from 1 lime over the calamari and set aside.

If your duro is not pre-puffed, pour the oil into a large Dutch oven until it's at least an inch deep. Heat the oil until it reads 350°F on a deep-frying thermometer. Using tongs, insert the duro into the hot oil. Using another set of tongs in your other hand, hold the edges of the duro down in the oil so that they don't curl up until fully puffed, about 2 minutes. Remove from the oil and drain on paper towels until cool.

Spread a layer of Mexican crema over the puffed duro. Cover it with a layer of lettuce or cabbage, followed by cucumber, tomatoes, red onion, and cheese. Drain the calamari and arrange over the top. Squirt Chamoy and the juice from the remaining lime over the top; sprinkle with chile-lime salt. To eat this snack, either break off chunks of the duro with toppings or pick it up and crunch into the whole thing.

Elotes (Street Corn on a Stick)

MAKES 6 SERVINGS

Elotes are sold by street vendors from trucks all over town. You will be handed an ear of corn spiked on one end with a popsicle stick and slathered in Mexican crema. You will be set free to cover that corn in the hot sauces, grated cheese, and seasonings of your choice from a selection of offerings. Use either fresh corn ears broken in half or frozen Nibblers, because popsicle sticks can break under the weight of a full ear. The corn on the cob is really just a crunchy, easy-to-hold vehicle for the creamy, salty, spicy, cheesy toppings and frozen works just as well due to its softer texture. Everybody's preferred cheese-to-chili-to-crema ratio is different, so for a party, follow the street vendors' lead and lay the toppings out for everyone to apply as they wish.

3 ears fresh corn, shucked and cut in half, or one 6-count package of frozen corn on the cob, such as Green Giant Nibblers

Sea salt

6 popsicle sticks or other firm skewers

1 lime or lemon

¼ cup mayonnaise

¼ cup unsweetened evaporated milk

1 chipotle in adobo sauce, chopped finely (about 1 tablespoon, optional)

1 tablespoon white vinegar

2 tablespoons chopped cilantro

Red chile powder to taste (New Mexico or cayenne)

½ cup crumbled Cotija cheese

Cook the fresh corn in a large pot of boiling, salted water until just tender, about 5 minutes. Or, cook the frozen corn according to package directions. Skewer one end with a popsicle stick. Cut the lime in half and squeeze the juice over the prepared corn.

In a small bowl, stir together the mayonnaise, evaporated milk, chipotle, and vinegar. Spread the mixture over the corn ears. Sprinkle evenly with cilantro, chile powder, salt to taste, and cheese, and eat.

VARIATION: MEXICAN STREET CORN IN A CUP

Cut the corn from the ears, then put in a bowl. Add the mayonnaise, evaporated milk, lime juice, chipotle, and 1 tablespoon melted butter, and mix well. Transfer to a cup and sprinkle with the cilantro, chile powder, salt, and cheese. Eat with a fork or spoon. You can experiment by adding chopped green chiles or shredded Monterey Jack cheese, if you like.

Sonoran-Style Pico De Gallo

MAKES 4 TO 6 SERVINGS

In other parts of the country, people only know of pico de gallo as a chunky fresh salsa. In Mexico and Tucson, pico de gallo also refers to spears of fresh fruit and/or vegetables sprinkled with chile powder, lime, and salt and served in 16-ounce party cups. Here is my favorite version.

1 fresh pineapple
1 large, fresh mango
½ medium-size watermelon
1 cucumber
1 medium jicama
6 Mexican limes or 3 large limes, halved
Pico de Gallo seasoning or Tajín
Sea salt to taste

Cut the top and bottom off of the pineapple, then cut away the peel, and cut lengthwise into spears. Peel the mango, slice in half lengthwise avoiding the pit, then slice into long wedges. Then cut the watermelon into spears similar in length to the pineapple, discarding the rind. Peel the cucumber and jicama and cut them into spears as well.

Fill plastic party cups with the fruit and vegetable spears. Squeeze over enough lime juice to cover everything. Then shake on lots of Pico de Gallo seasoning and salt to taste. Eat with a fork, then drink the spicy juice left at the bottom.

Paletas de Aguacate y Piña (Avocado and Pineapple Ice Pops)

MAKES 6 TO 8 ICE POPS

Avocados are a popular ingredient in paletas, handmade Mexican ice pops that come in every imaginable flavor combination. They are sold in snack shops and from tiny handcarts pushed around town by ancient, hunched proprietors. Here, pineapple and almond milk provide sweetness without added sugar, and I added fun flower-shaped sprinkles, which are made by Wilton. You'll need an ice pop mold for these eye-catching desserts.

1¼ cups pineapple chunks, fresh, frozen, or canned (drain if canned), divided

Sprinkles of your choice

2 limes

1 ripe avocado

¼ cup almond milk

6 to 8 popsicle sticks

Drop a few small chunks of pineapple, reserving some and a pinch of sprinkles into the bottom of each ice pop mold. Squeeze the juice from the 2 limes directly into a blender. Cut the avocado in half lengthwise, remove the pit, and scoop the flesh out. Add it to the blender. Add the remaining pineapple chunks and the almond milk to the blender. Blend on high speed until completely combined.

Spoon the blended mixture evenly over the pineapple chunks and sprinkles in the ice pop molds; follow the manufacturer's instructions to add the sticks and secure the mold. Freeze until firm, 4 to 6 hours or overnight.

Sweet Corn Paletas

MAKES 6 TO 8 ICE POPS

Why isn't corn used in more desserts? It's naturally sweet, and the kernels add a nice pop to these paletas. Have ready an ice pop mold with 6 to 8 wells to make these festive treats. There is a popular sweet drink called Atole sold by street vendors that's made with corn masa and flavored with cinnamon, which served as inspiration for this flavor combination.

1 teaspoon unsalted butter
2 cups corn kernels, divided
1 cup milk, any variety
1 cup half-and-half
¼ cup sugar
1½ teaspoons ground cinnamon
1 teaspoon vanilla extract
⅛ teaspoon kosher salt
⅔ cup plain Greek yogurt
6 to 8 popsicle sticks
1 tablespoon Pico de Gallo
　seasoning

Melt the butter in a medium saucepan over medium heat. Add 1 cup of the corn and sauté until browned, stirring occasionally, 7 to 10 minutes. Transfer to a small bowl.

Add the remaining 1 cup corn, milk, half-and-half, sugar, 1 teaspoon of the cinnamon, the vanilla, and salt to the saucepan. Cook over medium heat, stirring frequently, about 15 minutes. Remove from heat and let cool for 10 minutes before stirring in the yogurt. Pour the mixture into a blender or food processor and blend until smooth.

Divide the browned corn evenly among ice pop molds. Spoon in the yogurt mixture; follow the manufacturer's instructions to add the sticks and secure the mold. Freeze until firm, 4 to 6 hours or overnight.

To serve, unmold the ice pops. Dip the ends briefly in water, then dip the moist ends in Pico de Gallo seasoning mixed with the remaining ½ teaspoon cinnamon.

Raspado Mangonada with Mango-Lime Granita

MAKES 4 SERVINGS

The name raspados comes from the word "raspar," which means "to scrape." The treat's construction process involves shaving frozen snowy flakes from a giant block of ice into a cup, then saturating it all with fruit and juice and/or sweet-and-sour Chamoy syrup. Salty-sweet tamarind candies are often sprinkled on top of that. Giant blocks of ice are hard to come by, but I realized that you could use the method for making granita and get similar results in your home freezer. A granita is juice combined with sugar, and then frozen and scraped. So, instead of pure shaved ice I am using a mango-lime granita as the base for the raspado, which I then top with fresh fruit, Chamoy, tamarind, and seasonings, as they do in the local treat shops.

FOR THE GRANITA

2 large ripe mangos, peeled and chopped (about 2 cups)

1½ cups water

Juice of 3 limes

2 tablespoons sugar

FOR THE TOPPING

Chamoy to taste

1 ripe mango, peeled and chopped into small chunks

Chile-lime salt to taste, such as Tajín

Tamarind candies, such as chunks or Serpentina

Lime wedges for garnish

To make the granita, blend the mango chunks, 1½ cups water, lime juice, and sugar in a blender. Pour the mixture into a large deep-sided metal or ceramic cake pan. Cover with plastic wrap and freeze for 2 hours, then scrape the mixture with a fork, forming icy flakes. Refreeze for another hour and then scrape again. Repeat every hour until all of the liquid turns into flaky, fluffy granules of ice, about 1 to 2 more cycles.

Put a cup of the granita into a tall glass. Season with Chamoy. Top with mango chunks, chile-lime salt, and tamarind candies. Garnish with a lime wedge.

Desserts

Chocolate and sugar are probably two of the most revered ingredients in the history of Tucson. Chocolate was treated like gold in pre- and post-Columbian Tucson and was brought up from the South to the region in special convoys. Later, both chocolate and sugar were brought up to Tucson by wagon train and later by the railroad.

The Spanish-introduced sweet breads were used in part to lure the Native Americans away from some violent ancient rituals and created new, less-violent rituals. There's now a thriving tradition of bread baking in the desert Southwest.

Desert Dessert Nachos

MAKES 2 TO 4 SERVINGS

It was inevitable that the omnipresent tortilla chip would make its way into desserts. These sweet baked flour tortilla triangles are served as a stand-alone dessert and are also frequently used as a pretty garnish for ice cream sundaes. They are a great way to use up flour tortillas that are on the verge of drying out.

8 to 10 (6-inch) flour tortillas

Vegetable oil cooking spray

2 tablespoons unsweetened cocoa powder

2 tablespoons cinnamon sugar (see sidebar)

½ cup prepared caramel sauce, warmed

1 cup mini chocolate chips

1 cup chopped candied nuts, such as walnuts, almonds, or pecans

Preheat the oven to 325°F. Using a pizza cutter, cut the flour tortillas into triangles or free-form shapes. Place on a parchment-lined baking sheet. Mist lightly with the oil spray, then sprinkle generously on both sides with cocoa powder and cinnamon sugar. Bake until brown and crispy, 10 to 12 minutes.

Transfer the baked tortilla pieces to a large platter and drizzle with the warm caramel sauce. Sprinkle with the mini chocolate chips and candied nuts and serve warm.

CINNAMON SUGAR

I make my cinnamon sugar using a 1:4 ratio of ground cinnamon to sugar. Feel free to alter the ratio if you prefer a stronger cinnamon flavor.

Lemon Tres Leches Poke Cake

MAKES 8 TO 10 SERVINGS

Tres Leches is the original poke cake. After the cake is baked, you poke holes in it with a skewer, then fills the holes with three different kinds of milk: sweetened condensed milk, evaporated milk, and heavy cream (the tres leches!). I modified this recipe from one that Carlotta Flores, the chef at El Charro Café, taught me years ago. My version is flavored with lemon and coconut oil, then covered in lemon-flavored cream cheese frosting and sprinkles. It's refreshing and very festive.

FOR THE CAKE
Nonstick cooking spray
3 large eggs
1 cup plain whole-milk Greek yogurt
1 cup granulated sugar
¼ cup lemon juice
1 teaspoon vanilla extract
1 teaspoon lemon extract
1½ cups self-rising flour
¼ cup melted coconut oil

FOR THE TRES LECHES
1 (14-ounce) can sweetened condensed milk
1 (12-ounce) can evaporated milk
1 cup heavy cream

FOR THE LEMON CREAM CHEESE FROSTING
8 ounces cream cheese, softened
¼ cup plain whole-milk Greek yogurt
½ cup powdered sugar
1 teaspoon lemon extract

2 tablespoons sprinkles for decorating

Preheat the oven to 350°F. Spray the inside of a 9-by-13-inch cake pan with nonstick cooking spray.

To make the cake, in a large bowl, whisk together the eggs, yogurt, sugar, lemon juice, vanilla extract, and lemon extract. Slowly whisk in the flour, then fold in the coconut oil with a rubber spatula. Pour the batter into the prepared cake pan. Bake until a wooden skewer comes out clean, 30 to 35 minutes. Let cool until slightly warm to the touch.

To make the tres leches mixture, whisk together the sweetened condensed milk, evaporated milk, and heavy cream. Using a skewer (a chopstick will also work), poke evenly spaced holes in the top of the warm cake. Pour the milk mixture slowly over the cake. Cool for another 30 minutes, then refrigerate the cake, covered, at least 4 hours or overnight.

When the cake is completely cool, make the frosting: Using an electric mixer, beat together the cream cheese, yogurt, powdered sugar, and lemon extract. Frost the cooled cake, then decorate with sprinkles.

Dark Chocolate and Coffee Figgy Pudding Cakes

MAKES 4 INDIVIDUAL CAKES

Spanish missionaries first planted figs here in the 1690s; they are considered a heritage plant. This recipe is based on some idealized version of Christmas Past I have formed via the popular carol. Dark, rich, and subtly sweet, the figs are offset by decadent cocoa flavors, making this a sophisticated and cozy winter dessert. For the full experience, I strongly suggest you serve these with some sort of digestif while sitting by a roaring fire.

½ cup whole milk

3 tablespoons unsalted butter, melted

1 large egg

1 teaspoon vanilla extract

½ cup all-purpose flour

¼ cup almond meal

¾ cup (packed) dark brown sugar, divided

2 tablespoons unsweetened dark cocoa powder, such as King Arthur's black cocoa powder

½ teaspoon kosher salt

½ teaspoon baking powder

½ teaspoon ground cinnamon

Pinch of cayenne pepper

1 cup strongly brewed black coffee

8 fresh figs, such as Black Mission

Powdered sugar for garnish

Preheat the oven to 350°F. Spray 4 large (8- to 10-ounce capacity) ramekins with nonstick cooking spray; place on a rimmed baking sheet.

In a medium bowl, whisk together the milk, melted butter, egg, and vanilla. In a large bowl, whisk together the flour, almond meal, ¼ cup of the brown sugar, cocoa powder, salt, baking powder, cinnamon, and a pinch of cayenne. Slowly add the milk mixture to the dry mixture and combine using a rubber spatula.

Pour the coffee into a small saucepan over medium heat. Stir in the remaining ½ cup of brown sugar and bring to a boil. Reduce the heat to medium and simmer, stirring constantly, until the sugar is dissolved, about 2 minutes.

Cut half of the figs into quarters. Fill each ramekin halfway with the cake batter. Push 4 fig quarters into each, then gently top with a whole fig. Spoon the coffee sauce around the whole fig, leaving about an ⅛-inch of space at the top of the ramekin. Bake until the cakes are firm, and a toothpick inserted into the cake comes out clean, 25 to 30 minutes. Remove from the oven and sprinkle with powdered sugar. Serve warm.

Pan de Muerto

MAKES 3 SMALL BREADS

This is a traditional, slightly sweet bread prepared for Dia de los Muertos (Day of the Dead), a festival honoring the souls of those who have died. The bread dates back to the time of the Spanish conquistadors, who used the heart-shaped bread as a stand-in for pre-existing Aztec rituals. The heart shape has been modified to a simple round bread with crosses of dough draped over the top to resemble bones, and a small ball of dough on top to emulate a skull. Some people may find making the bones challenging to construct, but they do not have to be perfect, they just have to get the idea across.

FOR THE DOUGH
3 cups all-purpose flour

⅓ cup granulated sugar

1 packet instant yeast (2 teaspoons)

½ cup whole milk, microwaved for about 20 seconds until lukewarm, but not hot

¼ cup unsalted butter, softened

2 large eggs, beaten

1 teaspoon ground cinnamon

1 teaspoon finely grated orange zest

½ teaspoon kosher salt

½ teaspoon ground aniseed

FOR THE TOPPING
2 tablespoons unsalted butter, melted

2 tablespoons granulated or brown sugar

½ teaspoon ground cinnamon

In a large bowl mix together flour, sugar, yeast, milk, butter, eggs, cinnamon, orange zest, salt, and aniseed until well combined. Knead with your hands on a lightly floured surface until a smooth dough forms, 1 to 2 minutes. Place the dough in a large bowl, cover with a clean, slightly damp dishcloth, and let rise until doubled in size, about 90 minutes.

Separate a quarter of the dough, put it in another bowl, cover, and refrigerate.

Line a baking sheet with a silicone baking mat or parchment paper. Shape the remaining dough into three equal balls. Place the balls at even intervals on the baking sheet. Cover again with the dishcloth and let rise for another 90 minutes. The dough will have approximately doubled in size.

Remove the dough you placed in the refrigerator. Break it into three even pieces. Then shape each piece into one slightly flattened ball for the "skull" and two long rope-like pieces for the "bones." Refrigerate the skull and dough pieces for another 10 minutes (this helps them retain their shape), then drape the ropes over the bread to form a cross, pinching them at ½-inch intervals to make them look gnarled. Place the skull piece on top where the bones cross.

Preheat the oven to 350°F. Bake the breads until golden brown and springy, 20 to 25 minutes. Remove from the oven and immediately brush with the melted butter. Mix together the sugar and cinnamon, then sprinkle by hand over the top of the breads. Transfer to a wire rack and cool completely before serving.

Papel Picado (Crunchy Tortilla Snowflakes)

MAKES 8 SNOWFLAKES

Papel picado means "perforated paper," and it's a popular folk-art craft in Tucson and Mexico. This edible version will brighten any winter holiday table. This is probably the only time I will recommend using those super-soft, fluffy, white, supermarket tortillas. Use fine-pointed scissors and the softest, freshest tortillas you can find so that they fold easily without cracking. Serve these as a dessert or appetizer, either alone or with crème fraiche for dipping.

8 (6-inch) extra-fluffy flour tortillas

Olive oil spray or 2 tablespoons olive oil

2 tablespoons colored sanding sugar, such as turquoise blue

2 tablespoons sprinkles, such as white jimmies, snowflake quins, or multicolored nonpareils

1 tablespoon coarse salt flakes, such as Maldon

½ cup crème fraiche, for serving (optional)

Position your oven racks in the top and bottom thirds of the oven and preheat to 325°F. Line 2 large baking sheets with parchment paper or a silicone sheet liner.

Fold each tortilla in half, then in half again, and then in half a third time to make a roughly triangular shape. Using fine-pointed scissors, cut away small triangles or semicircles from the tortilla layers. Cut off a small piece from the tip, too, if you want a hole in the very center. Carefully unfold the tortillas—they will resemble large snowflakes—place them flat on the baking sheets, and spray or brush with olive oil.

Decorate the "snowflakes" to your liking with sanding sugar, sprinkles, and coarse salt. Bake until slightly golden around the edges, 8 to 10 minutes, switching and rotating the baking sheets halfway through. Serve with crème fraiche.

Index

Note: Page references in *italics* indicate photographs.

Acknowledgments

I am deeply grateful for all of the incredible folks who helped make this book possible. Creating a cookbook is a group project, and I was so lucky to have an amazing team working behind the scenes to bring this dream to fruition.

Thank you to all of the people who were there to support me along the way:

To my INCREDIBLE editor and publisher Jennifer Newens, who knows more about cookbook publishing than just about anyone; your help and support was invaluable. And thank you to the rest of the fabulous team at West Margin Press: editor Olivia Ngai, copy editor Charlotte Beal, and book designer Rachel Metzger.

To the contributing chefs: Maria Mazon, Travis Peters, Janos Wilder, Amanda Horton, Don Guerra, Benjamin Galaz, Gary Hickey, Suzana Davila, Patricia Schwabe, Isela Mejia, Daniel Contreras, Bruce Yim, Teresa and the Matias family, and grill master Bryan Keith. And a very special thank you to Carlotta Flores for everything that she has taught me over the many years that I have known her. Without her, and the whole Flores family, this book would have never been possible.

To Jonathan Mabry, Ph.D. and the folks at the Center for Regional Food Studies at the University of Arizona and to Chris Iglesias and Chris Swenson on behalf of Cacique dairy products.

To my husband, Jason Willis, who along with my two supportive and loving cats, Nova and Hawthorne, make home the very best place to be.

To my mother, Lois Ungar, and my brother, Jonathan Alpers, who helped set the foundation for a life of cooking and eating.

To my key editorial collaborators over the years: Sara Levine and Erin Hartigan from the Food Network, Elettra Wiedemann and Zoe Bain from *Refinery29*, Diane Kashy from Madden Publishing, Megan Kimball and Doug Biggers from *Edible Baja Arizona*, and Dan Gibson at *Visit Tucson*.

My dear friends Melanie Sutton, Helen Bernard, Andrea Turner, Ken & Deborah, and my original co-explorer of a new land, Andy Meinig.

And finally, thanks to this town. The desert.